INSIDE THATCHER'  ION

Inside Thatcher's Monetarist Revolution

Gordon Pepper
Professor
Department of Banking and Finance
City University Business School
London

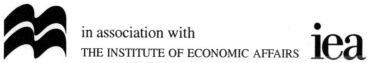

in association with
THE INSTITUTE OF ECONOMIC AFFAIRS iea

First published in Great Britain 1998 by
MACMILLAN PRESS LTD
Houndmills, Basingstoke, Hampshire RG21 6XS and London
Companies and representatives throughout the world

A catalogue record for this book is available from the British Library.

ISBN 0–333–71839–9 hardcover
ISBN 0–333–72012–1 paperback

First published in the United States of America 1998 by
ST. MARTIN'S PRESS, INC.,
Scholarly and Reference Division,
175 Fifth Avenue, New York, N.Y. 10010

ISBN 0–312–21040–X

Library of Congress Cataloging-in-Publication Data
Pepper, Gordon T., 1934–
Inside Thatcher's monetarist revolution / Gordon Pepper.
     p.   cm.
Includes bibliographical references and index.
ISBN 0–312–21040–X (cloth)
1. Monetary policy—Great Britain—History—20th century.
2. Great Britain—Economic policy—1945–   3. Economic forecasting–
–Great Britain.   I. Title.
HG939.5.P346 1998
332.4'941—dc21   97–28271
                                                          CIP

© Gordon Pepper 1998

This book is printed on paper suitable for recycling and made from fully managed and sustained forest sources.

10   9   8   7   6   5   4   3   2
07   06   05   04   03   02   01   00   99   98

Printed and bound in Great Britain by
Antony Rowe Ltd, Chippenham, Wiltshire

To my children: Alasdair, Ninna, Harry and Mark

Contents

List of Tables

List of Charts

Foreword

Many economists now subscribe to 'monetarism' in its various forms. But, in Britain twenty five years ago, monetarists were regarded as a fringe group set apart from a mainstream still dominated by Keynesian ideas. Economic policy-makers still attempted 'fine-tuning', albeit with little success, and almost all economic models had structures which were explicitly or implicitly Keynesian.

That monetarism has risen from obscurity to its present prominence is due to the persistence of a few economists who, in the 1970s and early 1980s, built on the foundations provided by academic economists such as Milton Friedman and Harry Johnson to provide a practical basis for policy. Gordon Pepper was a key member of the few.

The *Greenwell Monetary Bulletin*, which Professor Pepper edited, had a degree of influence in the City and with the government which no comparable publication had previously attained and which has certainly not been matched since. From the early 1970s, it attracted the attention of politicians, civil servants and Bank of England officials as well as other City institutions. Particularly during Mrs Thatcher's period of office, the status of the *Bulletin* was such that Pepper became an 'insider' with a remarkable opportunity to observe at close quarters the formation of economic policy during a period of radical change. He was also well placed to influence policy, even if he might often have disapproved of what the government did in the name of 'monetarism'.

Pepper's role in the 'monetarist revolution' places him in a unique position to write this book on the subject. In *Inside Thatcher's Monetarist Revolution* he has produced a masterly critical account of a fascinating and revealing period in British postwar economic history, beginning from the early days and showing how he and others at Greenwell worked out for themselves how monetarist ideas could be applied. Most of the book is accessible to people with an interest in economics, even if they lack formal qualifications, because of the care which Pepper takes in explaining the sources and the development of monetarist ideas and the way policy was applied. His analysis shows that monetarism apparently did not work for the same reason other economic policies often appear to fail – because they become politicised in implementation. In this case, the main tenets of monetarism were ignored, money supply was not controlled and politicians concentrated instead on unsuccessful attempts to manage expectations in financial markets. Professor Pepper spices his analysis with numerous anecdotes which lighten the tale and lend substance to his view that, far from monetarism having failed, it has not been tried.

Another contribution which this book makes to the literature is its analysis (in Part II) of the forecasting records of the main macroeconomic models of the British economy, including the extent to which they gave forewarning of seven major economic events (four recessions and three inflations). Professor Pepper treads carefully in this difficult area of comparing forecasts with outcomes but concludes that, in general, the main models 'did little better than predict events as they started to occur'. The record of the Greenwell monetarist approach, however, appears better: the seven major events were predicted, although (inevitably) forecasts of timing were often awry.

The last four chapters discuss more recent events of special interest to monetary economists. They deal with the formation of the 'Liverpool Six', the policy disagreements which have broken out among monetarists (particularly about the relative significance of broad money and narrow money) and the forecasting records of individual monetary economists. The results of Pepper's many years of experience are distilled into two chapters where he sets out his own views on monetary analysis (Chapter 11) and on the policy implications of the book (Chapter 13).

A previous book by Gordon Pepper[*] proved to be one of the Institute of Economic Affairs' best-sellers, appealing to a wide audience attracted by its ability to explain complex ideas to non-specialists. *Inside Thatcher's Monetarist Revolution* has similar appeal. As with all publications in which the Institute is involved, the conclusions are those of the author, not of the Institute (which has no corporate view), its Trustees, Advisers or Directors. But economists, historians, political scientists – indeed anyone interested in the sources of ideas and how those ideas are developed – will find stimulating original materials in this book.

COLIN ROBINSON
Professor of Economics, University of Surrey
Editorial Director, Institute of Economic Affairs

---

[*] Gordon Pepper, *Money, Credit and Inflation: An Historical Indictment of UK Monetary Policy and a Proposal for Change*, Research Monograph 44, Institute of Economic Affairs, Second Impression, 1991.

Introduction and Summary

Part I of this book starts with the history of monetarism in the UK in the early 1970s. Three people started to write regular commentaries. They were Alan Walters, now Sir Alan, who became Mrs Thatcher's personal economic adviser when she was Prime Minister, Brian Griffiths, now Lord Griffiths, who became head of the Prime Minister's Policy Unit, and the author, who stayed in the private sector and became joint senior partner of the stockbrokers W. Greenwell & Co. and, later, chairman of Greenwell Monatagu.

The author was the primary editor of the *Monetary Bulletin* which was circulated by W. Greenwell & Co. well into the 1980s and became most influential. The book describes how Greenwell became the centre of a network of economists in the City, which at times included the Bank of England (the Bank), and how possible contents of a *Bulletin* were often discussed widely in the gilt-edged market, so much so that on occasions a *Bulletin* came to express the views of the market itself.

Chapter 2 describes the learning curve at Greenwell; in particular how Keynesian and monetarist forecasts of the economy were reconciled; how mistakes were found in first one and then the other; how explanations for the behaviour of the money supply were always sought; and how differences between the various monetary aggregates were investigated. It also describes early work monitoring the public sector borrowing requirement, the financial surpluses and deficits of the various sectors of the economy and what came to be described as the 'real balances effect'. The chapter also discusses some of the problems associated with becoming a 'guru', the reaction of clients and the relationship with the Bank.

The *Monetary Bulletin* attracted the attention of politicians as well as officials. In the early 1970s it was drawn to the attention of Anthony Barber, when he was Chancellor of the Exchequer and Edward Heath was Prime Minister. During the following Labour Government the author had contact with both Harold Wilson and Denis Healey as well as numerous Conservatives. Chapter 3 describes how he then became an unofficial adviser to Margaret Thatcher when she was leader of the Opposition and a 'fly on the wall' during the Thatcher revolution.

Chapter 4 discusses the outcome of monetarism in the 1980s when Mrs Thatcher was Prime Minister. It distinguishes between monetary control for its own sake and how monetary targets could be used for political purposes, for example to manage expectations in financial markets. The former was never tried in earnest. The latter was a complete failure, as is usual with public relations exercises that are not based on reality. Various other reasons for monetarism falling into disrepute are discussed.

As the money supply was not controlled the validity of monetarism cannot be judged from an experiment with monetary control in the 1980s. It is suggested that the next strongest test is whether forecasts of the economy based on monetary analysis were better or worse than conventional ones.

Part II examines forecasting records. It starts with a brief history of macroeconomic modelling and how the three main models of the UK economy are those of London Business School (LBS), the National Institute of Economic and Social Research (NIESR) and the Treasury (HMT). The author was involved with macroeconomic modelling in two ways. First, the Centre for Economic Forecasting at LBS was sponsored by a consortium of companies. The original idea was that there should be one firm from each industry; W. Greenwell & Co. were the stockbrokers. As a representative of Greenwell the author attended nearly all of the meetings in the 1970s when Jim Ball and Terry Burns were running the model.[1] This gave him an excellent insight into the performance of the model.

The second way in which the author was involved with macroeconomic modelling was with the provision of public finance for modelling. Most of the funds are channelled through the Macroeconomic Modelling Consortium (consisting of the Economic and Social Research Council (ESRC), the Treasury and the Bank). The author was on the council of the ESRC from 1989 to 1993 and chairman of the Consortium from 1991 to 1994. He learnt a great deal about the performance of the models from this experience in spite of not being a modeller himself.

The accuracy of economic forecasts is discussed in Chapter 6. The margin of error is greater than one percentage point of GDP, no matter whether the forecast is Keynesian or monetarist and whether or not use is made of a macroeconomic model. Because of the inaccuracy it is argued that forecasters should *not* attempt to predict minor variations in the business cycle and that they should concentrate instead on trying to predict major events that should be within the margin of accuracy of their techniques.

The reason why forecasters continue to make routine forecasts is that they will not receive publicity if they do not do so, and there is a danger that a forecast of a major event, which by its nature will be made only occasionally, will pass unnoticed. Further, forecasters will not be able to obtain sponsorship if they do not produce a regular product. It is argued that persistence with routine forecasts in spite of their inaccuracy is an example of market failure.

Chapter 7 defines major economic events, starting with the four recessions and the three inflations since 1969. Chapter 8 examines the records of LBS, NIESR and the Treasury. Each of the seven events is studied and the first warnings of an event are identified. The LBS, for example, publishes its first forecast of a particular year 36 months prior to the start of the year. This forecast and the succession of subsequent forecasts can be examined to find out when the first warning of an event during a year was sounded. For ease of reading, the detailed analysis is given in appendices, with the results summarised in the text of the chapter. The conclusion is that forecasts using macroeconomic models did little better than predict events as they started to occur.

Chapter 9 examines the forecasting record of the monetarist approach developed at Greenwell. The library of *Monetary Bulletins*, articles and speeches by the author consists of over 350 items. Unlike LBS, NIESR and the Treasury Greenwell never published routine forecasts, for the reason given earlier. This means that the whole library has to be scrutinised rather than a table of forecasts. Again for ease of reading, the detailed scrutiny is contained in an appendix, with the results summarised in the text. Analysis of the seven major events is a fairly simple task; all of them were predicted to a greater or lesser extent but not their precise timing. A more difficult assignment is to trace erroneous predictions of events that did not occur. Forecasters tend to remember their successes but forget their failures and the author is no exception. Overall, the conclusion is that the record of the monetarist approach developed at Greenwell was significantly better than that of the macroeconomic models. This is evidence of the validity of monetarism.

The evidence advanced in Chapter 9 includes warnings about the 1990/92 recession sounded by the 'Liverpool Six' in letters to *The Times*, as the author was one of the Six. These letters received considerable publicity in 1991 and 1992 before the UK was forced out of the Exchange Rate Mechanism of the European Monetary System. Chapter 10, the first chapter in Part III, describes the formation of the Six and how its members had broken away from the Shadow Monetary Policy Group. Professors Tim Congdon and Patrick Minford were members of both bodies, played key roles and subsequently became 'wise men' appointed by Norman Lamont when he was Chancellor of the Exchequer. It might be thought that these two monetarists would agree with each other but this is not the case, their main disagreement being about the relative importance of narrow and broad money. Argument between them in public helped to bring monetarism into disrepute in the UK. The author tried to mediate between them when he was chairman of the Shadow Monetary Policy Group, and he benefited greatly from the discussion that ensued. Chapter 11 describes the lessons the author learnt about monetary analysis from this discussion and from thirty years' practical experience.

Having described the differences between Congdon and Minford Chapter 12 discusses their forecasting records. Congdon's is good but relatively short. His method is similar to the author's although he has extended it further. It is suggested that Congdon's and the author's forecasting records taken together cover a sufficiently long span of time to be firm evidence of the validity of monetarism.

The concluding Chapter 13 sets out some of the policy implications of the analysis in the book.

SUGGESTIONS FOR READING THE BOOK

Some of the sections of the book are written primarily for specialists of various persuasions. A generalist reading the book for the first time should have read this Introduction and Summary. He, or she, should then merely glance at Chapter 1, about early monetarism in the UK, before moving on to Chapter 2. The next chapter to skim through is Chapter 5 which contains a brief history of macroeconomic models. Moving on to Chapter 8, a glance at the beginning of Appendices 8.1 and 8.2, containing the detailed analysis of the forecasts emanating from the models, should be sufficient to give an idea of the type of analysis. Similarly the Appendix of Chapter 9 may be dipped into to give a flavour of the forecasts contained in the Greenwell *Monetary Bulletin* rather than read in full. Chapter 11, entitled 'The Current State of Knowledge', may be omitted, at any rate on a first reading.

Many generalists will be interested in politics, the political process and the workings of Whitehall and Westminster. They should find Chapters 2, 3 and 4 of particular interest. Attention is drawn to the notes because they often contain anecdotes, for example Note 5 of Chapter 3 describes how the author was approached after Labour had lost the election in 1979 to find out if he would be prepared to brief Mr Callaghan in the same way as he had Mrs Thatcher when she was leader of the Opposition.

In spite of what has just been advised about glancing at sections of the book the author hopes that the parts of the book designed for specialists will be of interest to generalists too. A story is relevant here. In 1989 the author spoke at a conference at which Tim Congdon and Patrick Minford were also speakers and they again argued in public. At the lunch which followed the author sat next to the Director of the Institute of Economic Affairs and expressed his irritation. The result was that he was commissioned to write a booklet to set the record straight. The result was *Money, Credit and Inflation* (Pepper 1990b). The author was very surprised to learn a few months later that the booklet had been chosen by the Oxford and Cambridge Examinations Board as a set document for A level Economics. Some schoolboys subsequently told him that it was much easier to read than many text books. The point of this story is that it is possible to write for experts and at the same time be intelligible to lay men. The author hopes that the same applies to the specialist sections of this book.

Historians who read the book should find the whole of Part I interesting. Revolutions in economic policy do not occur often. An interesting question is why new ideas are implemented when they are. The author was lucky enough to have a bird's eye view of the Thatcher revolution. The description of the 'Liverpool Six' in Chapter 10 may also be of interest and so may Chapter 1 which gives some of the history of early monetarism in the UK. (Chapter 5 merely summarises the history of macroeconomic models given in more detail elsewhere.)

Specialists who are Keynesians or macroeconomic modellers should make a special study of Chapter 8, including its appendices. As explained above the focus of attention is on forecasting major events. Appendix 8.1 examines sequences of forecasts for years in which events occur. Appendix 8.2 contains a different type of analysis; it compares predictions made a fixed period ahead, for example six months prior to the year being forecast, with the outturns. The author also hopes that Keynesians will study the Greenwell record in Chapter 9 to decide for themselves if the approach has something to offer.

Keynesians should also study Chapter 4 about the politics of money supply targets. Attention is drawn to attempts to managed expectations (particularly confidence), to the description of vested interests and to the example of an industry capturing its regulators. The last can happen in spite of ex-practitioners who have become regulators being people of great personal integrity, because they have often absorbed the culture of their industry during their working lives without realising the degree to which they have become biased.

Specialists who are monetarist will want to study the Appendix of Chapter 9 containing the survey of the predictions of the monetarist approach developed at Greenwell. Chapter 11, entitled 'The Current State of Knowledge', is designed for them. It is packed with the lessons the author has learnt from practical experience of trying to forecast the economy from the behaviour of the monetary aggregates. It is then well worth returning to Chapter 9 because its appendix contains many illustrations of the learning curve. The author does not claim that the lessons are all valid in today's changing circumstances. The reader can pick and choose for him or herself.

REFERENCES TO PAGE NUMBERS

There are numerous references in the book to page numbers. Some of them apply to this book and others to a *Monetary Bulletin* that is being considered. To avoid confusion a section number as well as a page number is given for the former. A page number without a section number applies to the latter.

REASONS FOR WRITING THE BOOK

This book has been written for three reasons. The main one is to correct the popular impression that monetarism was tried in the 1980s and failed. This is not so. It was not tried. Some painful economic experiences can be avoided in the future if the policy prescriptions in the concluding Chapter 13 are followed. Secondly, the author thinks that he has learnt a lot from close observation of the financial scene and from practical experience, and that the approach developed at W. Greenwell & Co. has something to offer. He wishes to pass on this experience to others. The third reason is that the author was lucky enough to be in the right place at the right time; he was close to the centre of action; and had a lot of fun. People who have read the account say that they have enjoyed it and have demanded more. They are primarily to blame for the inclusion of anecdotes!

Acknowledgements

The author would like to thank Forrest Capie, Michael Finley, Laurence Gooderham, Terry Mills, Colin Robinson, Anthony Seldon, Adrian Sycamore, Alan Walters and Geoffrey Wood for reading drafts of the book and for helpful comments. Any errors that remain are of course his own responsibility.

PART I

How the Monetarists Came to Power

1 Early Monetarism in the UK

1.1 THE MONEY STUDY GROUP

Monetarism in its modern form first came to prominence in the UK in the early 1970s after Harry Johnson (London School of Economics and Chicago), David Laidler (Essex), Bob Nobay (LSE and Southampton) and Michael Parkin (Essex) decided in 1967 to organise a conference to commemorate the tenth anniversary of the Radcliffe Report (1959) on the workings of the UK monetary system. The conference was held in Hove in 1969, its proceedings being published in *Money in Britain* (Croome and Johnson 1970). Among other things it was decided to form a discussion group called the Money Study Group. Funding was obtained from the Social Sciences Research Council, renamed the Economic and Social Sciences Research Council in 1984. Other conferences followed the one in Hove. A second was held in Sheffield in September 1970, the proceedings of which were published in *Monetary Theory and Monetary Policy in the 1970s* (Clayton *et al.* 1971). A third was held in London in January 1971 and the proceedings published in *The Current Inflation* (Johnson and Nobay 1971).

The Money Study Group still exists (in 1997). It meets regularly and holds annual conferences, although its name has been changed to the Money, Macro and Finance Research Group.

1.2 THE MANCHESTER INFLATION WORKSHOP

The Manchester Inflation Workshop was formed by David Laidler and Michael Parkin in the early 1970s, after they had moved from Essex to Manchester. Although it did not produce regular forecasts it became a centre for monetary analysis in the UK, much of which was published in the *Manchester School* (see Congdon 1992a: 23, 28–30, 101 and 222). Laidler and Parkin subsequently emigrated to North America and were succeeded by Michael Artis.

1.3   ALAN WALTERS

Another economist who was to become most prominent was Alan Walters (now Sir Alan). In 1967 he was still at Birmingham where he specialised in transport economics.[1] Rather surprisingly he was not one of the founders of the Money Study Group.

In autumn 1968 Walters moved to LSE. He also worked part-time for the Central Policy Review Staff (CPRS, a 'think tank' headed by Victor Rothschild). In *Path to Power* Margaret Thatcher (now Lady Thatcher) describes him as 'a brilliant, but little-known, monetary economist ... [who] resigned from the CPRS and delivered not only a scathing criticism of the Government's approach [in 1972] but also accurate predictions of where it would lead' (Thatcher 1995: 221). He also wrote the *Sebag Gilt Edged Review* (Joseph Sebag was a leading stockbroker at that time) which included the criticisms and predictions (see Walters 1986: 114).

Walters became close to Mrs Thatcher but he moved to Washington in 1975 shortly after she became leader of the Conservative Party, which was then in opposition. In November 1980 he came back to the UK as adviser to the Prime Minister after the Conservatives had been returned to power. In mid-1984 he returned to live in Washington and travelled regularly between there and London as a part-time adviser. In May 1989 he came back to London to become a full-time adviser to the Prime Minister once again, before resigning in October 1989 after Nigel Lawson's (now Lord Lawson) resignation as Chancellor of the Exchequer.

1.4   BRIAN GRIFFITHS

Another monetary economist was Brian Griffiths (now Lord Griffiths). In 1968 he was Lecturer in Economics at LSE. He became Professor of Banking and International Finance at City University Business School in 1977 and also director of the Centre for Banking and International Finance. For a time he wrote a review for the gilt-edged stockbrokers Pember and Boyle. In 1982 he became Dean of the Business School before moving on in 1985 to become the head of the Prime Minister's Policy Unit at 10 Downing Street.

1.5   CHARLES GOODHART

Yet another influential monetary economist was Charles Goodhart. In 1967 he was Lecturer in Monetary Economics at LSE. In 1969 he joined the Bank of England as an adviser with particular reference to monetary policy. He remained at the Bank until he returned to LSE in 1985.

1.6 PETER JAY

Peter Jay should also be mentioned. In 1967, after a spell in the Treasury, he became economics editor of *The Times* and frequently gave prominence to monetary analysis, before leaving in 1977 to become UK ambassador in Washington.

1.7 REGULAR PUBLICATIONS AND FORECASTS

Two regular reviews have been mentioned, the *Sebag Gilt Edged Review*, written by Alan Walters, and *Pember & Boyle's Review*, written by Brian Griffiths. A third was the *Monetary Bulletin*, circulated by stockbrokers W. Greenwell & Co., of which the author was the principal editor.[2]

The Greenwell *Monetary Bulletin* was circulated for many more years than the other two reviews and became most influential. This is illustrated by the author being voted the leading gilt-edged analyst throughout the 1970s.[3] Being one of the original 'teenage scribblers' might not seem important to some, but the authorities paid attention because of the influence one might have on the gilt-edged market, especially as the market's behaviour had on more than one occasion forced a government to change policy.[4] In *The Path to Power* Mrs Thatcher writes:

> Indeed, over the whole of this period – whether in 1956, 1966 or above all in 1976 – real cuts in public spending were only made by governments of either party under the exigent circumstances of a sterling crisis, a gilt strike or the arrival on the scene of the International Monetary Fund. (Thatcher 1995: 140)

The authorities presumably thought that the author might influence a gilt strike. But the *Monetary Bulletin* became more than this. As will be explained, Greenwell became the centre of a network of financial economists in the City. Possible contents of a *Bulletin* were often discussed widely in the gilt-edged market, so much so that on occasions it came to express the view of the market itself. The next chapter tells the story of the research project at Greenwell and how the *Bulletin* evolved.

2 Greenwell's *Monetary Bulletin*

2.1 THE RADCLIFFE REPORT

The starting point of the research project at W. Greenwell & Co. was the publication in 1959 of the report of the Radcliffe Committee on the Workings of the Monetary System. One of the recommendations was that more financial statistics should be published. Accordingly, in 1960 the Bank of England (the Bank) started its *Quarterly Bulletin* and in 1962 the Central Statistical Office began its monthly *Financial Statistics*. Both were of limited use at first. Coverage of data was gradually extended but, as with most other statistics, trends were often more important than absolute values and it took time to build up adequate series of past data. In 1967 we, that is, the author and the team at Greenwell, judged that sufficient data had become available to warrant a thorough investigation into their possible use for gilt-edged investors.

2.2 THE RESEARCH PROJECT

The history of Greenwell's research project up to the start of the *Monetary Bulletin* was published in *Too Much Money...?* (Pepper and Wood 1976: 49–56). Briefly, every statistic mentioned in the Bank's *Quarterly Bulletin* was graphed (which had to be done by hand in those days), with the horizontal scale for time the same in all graphs. The Bank's comments were written on each graph, opposite the relevant date. Each graph was compared with the ones for interest rates, using a draughtsman's light-box, to see if there were any leads or lags, especially at the major turning points. The graphs were then hung all over the walls of a room where they could be 'eyeballed' in combination. In modern parlance the aim was to establish a leading indicator of gilt-edged prices.

The interim conclusions were complicated and disappointing. Indicators had to be composite to be of any use, consisting of at least three statistics; typically one statistic needed to be confirmed by another, and a third must not be pointing in the opposite direction. More basically, different indicators had to be used according to the phase of the gilt-edged market. For example the set used in a bull market to indicate that it was likely to continue was of little use at other times. A second set had to be used as the bull market became mature to warn that a turning point was about to take place. A third one had to be used in the subsequent bear market to indicate that it was likely to continue and, as that market became mature, a fourth set had to be used to warn of a new turning point. Knowing whether one was in a bull or bear market, and whether the market was mature or not, begged much of the question.

The main benefit of the research project came when we realised that all the hard work carrying out the historical analysis had greatly increased our understanding of the market. One example was realisation that the flow of funds of the banking sector had a major influence on gilt-edged prices. These flows of funds can be defined as the growth of the deposits that banks take less the loans that they make, the balance being available for investment or disinvestment as the case might be. There was a connection between this and clearing banks' purchases and sales of gilt-edged stock. We found that such transactions tended to dominate the gilt-edged market when banks were in substantial financial imbalance (explained in Pepper 1994: 29–40). This drew our attention to liquidity and flow of funds in general.

2.3 INTRODUCTION TO MONETARISM

A landmark occurred in June 1968 when I attended a seminar organised by the US Financial Analysts Federation and met Dr Beryl Sprinkel. (The first person is used as the account becomes more personal.) Sprinkel was an ardent monetarist, then with Harris Trust and Savings Bank and later one of the chairmen of the Council of Economic Advisors who served under President Reagan. I was impressed by the record of accurate forecasts that he had documented. He used monthly data for the money supply and on my return home we started to derive similar data for the UK from the monthly returns of clearing banks held in the library of the Institute of Bankers. We had made several months' progress by the time the UK had to resort to the IMF in October 1968. When the IMF's delegation arrived in London on the fifteenth of that month we telephoned the Bank to let them know about our data. Someone came round straight away, but we gained the impression that he had difficulty understanding our research project. (The Bank subsequently recruited Charles Goodhart as already reported.)

After the visit of the IMF the money supply became topical. Our first note on the subject was circulated on 18 October, only three days after the delegation arrived. Our second note was circulated on 5 November 1968.

2.4   *COMPETITION AND CREDIT CONTROL*

The next landmark came in 1971 when the Bank decided to change the UK's system of monetary control. A consultative document, *Competition and Credit Control*, was published in May of that year. One of the proposals was publication of monthly data for the money supply. The official publication *Banking Statistics* started in March 1972. The first edition of the *Monetary Bulletin* followed in June 1972.

2.5   THE TIMING OF THE RELEASE OF *BANKING STATISTICS*

For some unknown reason the Bank released the monthly data for the money supply at 10.30 a.m., in contrast to most official statistics, which are released later in the day. This turned out to be important for us at Greenwell because it gave us time to analyse the data and get copies of a *Monetary Bulletin* to the press before journalists wrote their news stories about the money supply. A reference to the *Bulletin* was often included in their reports. The result was that the *Bulletin* received a great deal of publicity, often on the front pages of quality newspapers.

2.6   A NETWORK OF FINANCIAL ECONOMISTS

The publicity had consequences. Economists throughout the City started to telephone us with queries about current financial data as they thought that we were an authority. Some times we could clarify a point but often we could not. We passed on the queries to others who telephoned. The result was that Greenwell became the centre of a web that originally consisted of John Atkins of CitiBank, Graeme Gilcrist of Union Discount, David Kearn of NatWest Bank, David Tapper of Hambros Bank, Brian Williams of Gerrard and National, and Peter Wood of Barclays Bank (Treasurer's Department). The query was often about why a rate of interest had changed, usually about why one rate had moved relative to others. People then started reporting unusual types of transaction to us. Being able to pick the brains and tap the first-hand knowledge of all these experts added greatly to our own expertise.

      The Bank also contributed to the network. I used to wait whilst we and others were addressing a problem and then report the investigation and the solution that had so far been worked out to the Bank. The economist to whom I talked was nearly always interested. If one listened carefully to his response one might be pointed in the right direction. Even a response like 'I do not think that is quite right' was of some use as it encouraged second thoughts. 'Have you thought of so and so?' was more helpful. In general a telephone call to the Bank asking them to explain something that was occurring in the marketplace usually received short shrift, but the Bank would often help with serious analysis. It was not in their interest for us to circulate erroneous comment.

2.7 FIRST-HAND KNOWLEDGE

It is worth stressing that Greenwell's position as a gilt-edged broker gave us an excellent overview of what was happening in the market for long-term savings. This was because gilt-edged stock are often a residual investment in the sense that any savings left over after attractive invest-ment opportunities have been taken up are often invested in the gilt-edged market. The size of such purchases may or may not be equal to the amount that the authorities need to sell and imbalances can be observed. At Greenwell we did not have the same first-hand knowledge of what was happening in the money market and it was here that the network of bank economists filled the gap.

There is a further point. In all recorded financial statistics purchases are always equal to sales because a transaction cannot take place without there being both a buyer and a seller; something cannot be sold unless someone buys it. The statement that the stock-market has fallen because of more selling than buying is nonsense. The statement should read that more people *intended* to sell than buy at the prevailing price. Official statistics record actual transactions and not intended ones.

At Greenwell we had a great advantage over economic historians subse-quently studying the data. Greenwell's share of turnover in the gilt-edged market grew to about 10 per cent and was sufficiently large for us often to know whether sellers or buyers were originating transactions. Suppose for example that intended buyers exceed intended sellers at the current price. When an intended buyer tries to purchase stock the price of the stock rises and this rise in price tempts a seller. The transaction is then executed. The buyer has originated the transaction and the seller has accommodated it. *We often knew the direction of causality from our own business.*

2.8 THE TEAM

I was the principal author of the *Monetary Bulletins* and responsible for originating most of the ideas but, as already explained, I remorselessly picked the brains of others throughout the City. The same applied within Greenwell.

The other author was Robert Thomas (whose initials, RLT, appeared on *Bulletins*). We both had Cambridge degrees in economics and had gone on to qualify as actuaries.[1] Robert's role was different from mine. He was superb, certainly better than me, at servicing Greenwell's dealing desks, warning them when an economic statistic was due to be published, giving some idea of expectations and producing an assessment very soon after publication. He was available to answer queries and support the expertise of Greenwell's salesmen. As far as *Bulletins* were concerned we developed the ideas together and he was also responsible for most of the statistical work and detail. Robert's role was vital.

The third member of the team that wrote the *Bulletin* was a consultant. At the time Robert and I did not think of ourselves as professional economists because neither of us had a formal postgraduate qualification in economics.[2] We were largely self-taught. The team needed supplementing by a professional economist. From our exposure to the Money Study Group we realised that whereas academics could argue about the various possible theoretical channels of transmission very few of them had a good grasp of which of channels were important in practice. Only economists from the Bank appeared to have a good idea of the size of the numbers. This suggested that we should try to recruit one of the Bank's economists, but poaching someone from the Bank was unheard of in those days. One of the recommendations of the Radcliffe Report however had been that the Bank should employ academic economists in its Economic Intelligence Department on two-year secondment. Geoffrey Wood (initials GEW) was among the first to finish such a secondment and we recruited him as soon as he left the Bank.[3] He fulfilled a most important role until he was seconded to the Federal Reserve Bank of St Louis in 1977.

Geoffrey's successor as consultant to the *Bulletin* was Dr Ray Richardson (initials RR) who we had met when he was adviser to the Chancellor of the Duchy of Lancaster, Harold Lever (the late Lord Lever), who had been made responsible for the gilt-edged market by the Chancellor of the Exchequer, Denis Healey (now Lord Healey) (see Healey 1989: 384). As consultant to the *Bulletin* Ray had the difficult task of curbing my enthusiasm to innovate and of turning early drafts into English. He had the knack of writing 'one-liners' that the press would quote, which was not surprising given his experience as a speech-writer for Harold Lever.

The team writing the *Bulletin* had a great deal of help from others in Greenwell. Three people in particular should be mentioned. Pip Greenwell, the senior partner, gave tremendous support and advice. Mike

Higgins was most thorough when reading for detail; successfully running the hurdle of his scrutiny gave us confidence. Laurence Gooderham read for general impression and perspective; changes were often made as a result of his comments.

John Olcay was another of my partners who merits special mention. He was our international partner. Before joining Greenwell he had been chief economist of the Bank of New York. As such he was a professional economist, with a post-graduate degree from Wharton, who was well known to many in both the US and elsewhere. I learnt to walk the corridors of power with him in the US, that is, the Treasury, the Council of Economic Advisors, the Office of the Management of the Budget and the Federal Reserve. He also introduced me to many in the Brookings Institute. I learnt a great deal from him. He was also a co-author of some of the *Bulletins*; for example he wrote the opening words of a memorable one commenting on the budget in April 1974: 'A balanced judgement of the budget and its influence on economic activity and financial markets would gain immeasurably from an exercise in marrying the economic forecasts of the Treasury with a flow of funds analysis (see Section A.9.1.3, p. 141; note that a reference giving a Section number as well as a page number applies to the present volume).' This may seem 'old hat' today but at the time it was novel.

2.9   THE EARLY *BULLETINS*

Various features stand out on rereading the early editions of the *Bulletin*. Firstly both Robert and I, having read economics at Cambridge, were brought up as Keynesians and in so far as we became monetarists we did so reluctantly and learnt as we went along. We argued at first that although monetarism might work in the US it was unlikely to do so in the UK because the two economies were very different. We stressed that the US, with exports only about 5 per cent of GNP, was a relatively closed economy in contrast to the openness of the UK where exports amounted to about 25 per cent of GDP. Another difference was the much larger size of the public sector in the UK (see Pepper 1970). We only abandoned this jaundiced view of monetarism after a monetarist forecast for the UK turned out to be more correct than the corresponding Keynesian one (see Section A.9.1.1, p. 139).

2.10   KEYNESIAN AND MONETARIST FORECASTS

Many US monetarists start their analysis with the behaviour of the money supply but we were never satisfied with this approach. We always wanted to find out why the money supply was behaving in the way it was. The explanation often made sense to Keynesians. The money supply for example is influenced by the public sector borrowing requirement and a change in this may indicate that something unexpected is happening to the stance of fiscal policy. Another example is that the money supply is affected by the amount of exports less imports (via its external component) and Keynesians agree that this influences economic activity.

We argued that both Keynesian and monetarist forecasts of the economy should be made and that they should then be reconciled (see for example the *Bulletin* in June 1973, 'A review of the Year', pp. 1, 6). If the forecasts do not agree both should be reworked until they do. The error in the Keynesian one may for example be in the assumptions, particularly about the level of savings. The error in the monetarist one may be that an aggregate is about to whiplash (that is, its rate of growth may be about to reverse sharply) or that the notoriously long and variable time lags between changes in monetary growth and the response of the economy have been wrongly estimated.

One type of error in a monetarist forecast merits special mention. There are various monetary aggregates (M1, M2, M3, M4, etc.) on which a forecast can be based. Each one of them has at times been distorted. To guard against this we learnt to monitor *all* the aggregates. If any of them is behaving in a peculiar way the reason should be ascertained. The explanation will often involve a change in one interest rate relative to another. The transactions responsible for the change in rates should be investigated, as should those in response to the change. Such an analysis adds greatly to one's understanding of what is happening in the financial system as a whole. In particular it discloses which aggregates are reliable and which are not.

The error disclosed by cross-checking the Keynesian and monetarist forecasts was sometimes in the former and sometimes in the latter. For example our Keynesian forecast was in error in 1972 whereas the monetarist one was wrong in 1974. Having reconciled the two types of forecast we tended to express the result in Keynesian rather than monetarist terms as this helped communication with a wider audience.

2.11   THE TRANSMISSION MECHANISM

One of the difficulties with monetarism is lack of clarity about exactly how changes in monetary growth affect the economy. The transmission mechanism has been described as a 'black box'. Surplus money can be spent in four ways:

(i)   on goods and services, in which case economic activity will accelerate;
(ii)   in a way which directly raises the price of goods and services, for example on a commodity, in which case inflation will rise;
(iii)   on non-sterling assets, for example sterling deposits may be exchanged for dollar ones, in which case sterling will tend to fall;
(iv)   on domestic assets, in which case stock market and property prices will tend to rise and the change in wealth will affect economic activity.

The first and second channels are stressed by all monetarists. We were probably unusual in the attention we paid to the fourth, but then we were stockbrokers and predicting the behaviour of capital markets was our main objective. The third channel is stressed by international monetarist (see Frenkel and Johnson, 1976) and we gave publicity to this in 1976 (see *Bulletin*, no. 52, May 1976, and no. 54, June 1976, extracts from which are given in Section A.9.1.4, p. 142). We were still learning lessons about the transmission mechanism when the *Bulletin* ceased to be published in 1989, for example that money resulting from loans to acquire domestic assets is likely to be spent on further acquisitions of such assets (as per the Lawson boom) whereas money resulting from loans to finance consumption is likely to be spent on goods and services (as per the Barber boom)(see Section 11.4.8, p. 171).

We also learnt that analysis of the financial deficits and surpluses of the various sectors of the economy (the public, overseas, corporate and personal sectors) could help to fill in the transmission mechanism. In particular we drew attention to the likely reaction of industrial companies if the corporate sector was facing a large deficit (see for example 'Financial Assessment After the Budget', April 1974, Section A.9.1.3, p. 141). Focus on changes in the real balances on the personal sector also helped (although we did not use the terminology that later became accepted; see *Bulletin* no. 52, April 1976).

Although our understanding of the transmission mechanism improved it remained inadequate. The real world has a capacity to surprise, and it is wise to be humble. Money, like water, will percolate through somewhere, but it may be impossible to predict where the spring will appear. I summed up the situation in a talk, 'The Use of Monetarism for Practical Working Economists', to the Society of Business Economists in October 1976. I compared money to water in a river. Suppose that the river flows into an ocean through a delta and that a great storm throws up a sand bar across the estuary. It is certain that the water in the river will eventually reach the ocean but it may be impossible to forecast the shape of the channels that will be gouged out. Some may be shallow, twist and turn whereas others may be deep and straight. The important point is that the water in the river must

sooner or later reach the ocean. With money this alone is often sufficient to
make a useful forecast. I asserted that it can be dangerous to try to predict
the main channel. The best one can do is to have some idea about what is
likely to happen and keep one's ear close to the ground to monitor the situation. The sound of rushing water confirms the channel being gouged out
(someone interrupted here with the words 'You get drowned!'). If one
cannot predict then one should at least be able to detect what is happening as
it happens and produce a rapid assessment of the implications.

2.12   SPEED OF PRODUCTION

A second feature apparent from rereading the early *Bulletins* is that they suffered from being written very quickly. They were circulated round the City
within minutes of being finished. Large Rank Xerox machines were on the
floor below my office and duplication usually started before a *Bulletin* was
completed, with a team of messengers standing by to deliver it by hand.[4]

The authorities eventually took over some of our analysis and they did it
much better. Early *Bulletins* contained some of the first detailed descrip-
tions of how markets worked, particularly the money market, which
prompted the Bank to publish more authoritative accounts in its *Quarterly
Bulletin*. Another example of pioneering was our discovery of monthly
data for the Consolidated Fund and the National Loans Fund (which were
published for legal reasons but received no publicity) which we used to
monitor the Public Sector Borrowing Requirement (PSBR). A very senior
official in the Treasury tried to discourage us from doing so. He told me
that the data were valueless and that the conclusions drawn in a *Bulletin*
were wrong. Subsequently the conclusions were proved right, possibly
thanks to luck rather than judgement. A little later the authorities started to
publish monthly data for the PSBR. We may have been the first, but our
efforts often appear crude by subsequent standards.

2.13   GURU STATUS

One of the results of publicity emanating from the *Bulletin* was that I
began to be described as a guru. The secret of becoming one is not merely
publishing good-quality analysis that predicts events reasonably accu-
rately. Of almost equal importance is knowing when a market will be
receptive to the analysis and to time the publication accordingly. I had two
desks. The first was in our gilt-edged dealing room. The second was in a

quiet room only a few feet away. I spent most of my time on the dealing desk talking to clients and in touch with the market. This greatly helped the timing of publication but things did not always turn out tidily. I can think of one occasion when a *Bulletin* went down like a lead balloon, with clients simply not interested in the analysis, but a week later it became one of the most topical.

The amount of press publicity often took me by surprise. The greater the intellectual content of a *Bulletin* the less appeared to be the publicity. A *Bulletin* with one simple theme usually attracted more attention. Another factor was the amount of competing news. A *Bulletin* that I thought was very newsworthy could easily be crowded out by something more important and might not be mentioned in the press at all. At other times it was apparent that journalists were searching to find something to write. Greenwell used to receive routine telephone calls at the close of business each day from journalists writing their market reports who wanted to know what had happened in the gilt-edged market during the day. News about a new *Bulletin* was often fed to them at the same time.

2.14   PRESSURE FROM CLIENTS

There were occasions when a client objected strongly to a *Bulletin*. I remember one when Pip Greenwell received a telephone call from a discount house to which we were the corporate broker. (Every quoted company had a broker, or brokers, as the official link between it and the Stock Exchange; Greenwell were the link for the particular discount house. More generally, stockbrokers could act for both issuers and investors. Issues were handled by a corporate finance department with a Chinese Wall around it to prevent the leak of confidential information.) The person making the call was the chairman of the discount house. He told Pip that two of his directors were listening to witness the conversation. He said that when the discount house was trading in gilts he did not mind competing against either market forces or the Bank, but he was damned if he was going to compete against Gordon Pepper at his own game. The gilt-edged market had just fallen because of publication of a *Bulletin* and it had cost the discount house a lot of money. The chairman of the discount house said that Greenwell, as their broker, was expected to be helpful and they should at least have been warned about the *Bulletin*. He threatened to sack us.

The above incident illustrates a dilemma when the *Bulletins* were thought to be moving markets. Some clients were not interested in the analysis in a *Bulletin*, but only wanted to know whether it was bullish or bearish and how the market was likely to react on publication. In today's parlance they wanted insider-trading information. Further, a client could be very upset if he thought that a competitor had been told about the contents of a *Bulletin* before he had. Telling everyone at the same time created an 'event' that could magnify the effect on the market. The situation was manageable if a change from being bullish to bearish, or vice versa, was gradual but this was not always the case. On one occasion I suddenly changed without giving my partners any warning, completely wrong-footing them, and became unpopular within the firm.

I began to wonder whether being a guru was compatible with being a stockbroker. I discussed the problem with Dr Henry Kaufman who, at the time, was the chief economist of Salomon Brothers in New York and a member of their management committee. Henry understood my problem. When he changed his position he had to publish the fact coast to coast. We tried to describe our decision-taking process to each other. Both of us had great respect for the views of those of our colleagues who were very close to the market and for the atmosphere in our dealing rooms. At times we might warn that financial forces were about to change and wait until the dealers' intuition confirmed the assessment, in which case there was not a conflict with our colleagues. On other occasions the confirmation did not come. The analytical case would grow stronger and eventually we took a decision to over-rule intuition. In my case it might not be a logical process; it could be an emotional reaction; that enough was enough. This could cause great difficulty for my partners. A few days later I could rationalise why I had become bearish, or bullish, as the case might be, but not at the time. Henry and I agreed that there was one difference between our two firms. When he changed without warning then the people who lost money were his partners and himself because they were market-makers; if I changed without warning then the people who lost money were Greenwell's clients, which meant that the damage to our business was longer lasting.

A solution to my problem was to talk about the contents of a *Bulletin* to a wide circle of clients and people within the gilt-edged market whilst the contents were being formulated. The result was that market reactions tended to occur before publication. Short-term speculators soon started to lose interest when they realised that publication of a *Bulletin* was no longer moving the market.

(Shortly afterwards Nigel Lawson started to shadow the Deutsche Mark and the problem disappeared because the timing of interest changes depended on sterling's exchange rate rather than on the behaviour of the money supply. Short-term operators in the gilt-edged market lost interest in the money supply almost completely when they realised what was happening.)

2.15   PRESSURE FROM THE BANK

The strange case of monetary policy
by William Keegan, Economics Correspondent

Scene: Threadneedle Street.
Time: The present.
Cast: Guide, assorted tourists and A Man from Greenwell's.

Guide: 'This is the Bank of England, the central bank. Its main function is to print money.'

Man from Greenwell's: 'You can say that again.'

It would be stretching things a bit to say that Mr Gordon Pepper, a partner in stock-brokers W. Greenwell, was conducting a one-man campaign against the Government's monetary policy. But nobody can deny that Mr Pepper's regular bulletins to clients are an important factor in the formation of City opinion on monetary trends; to quote one bank of England official not so long ago: 'Things are quiet at the moment. Gordon Pepper has the flu.'

Financial Times, 3 May 1973

The *Bulletin* often criticised official policy. In the mid-1980s the retiring chief-general manager of one of the clearing banks told me that I would not have been allowed to be so critical of the Bank if I had been their economist because the Bank had a great deal of patronage. What people did not realise was that some of the *Bulletins* that were most critical of official policy were actually helpful to officials. My arguing in public the case that they were arguing in private strengthened their hand; as they put it, they had a public hook on which to hang their hat.

A *Bulletin* was not always considered to be 'helpful'. One of them disclosed the history of the amount of gilt-edged stock that the Bank had sold and the level of the market at which the sales had been made. The theme was that it did not pay investors to bargain-hunt while the market was falling, the better strategy being to wait and apply for the first new issue after the market had turned upwards. The *Bulletin* disclosed how the Bank

had always allowed the 'bears to get back in'. A draft was sent to the
Bank. The executive director in charge of domestic monetary policy came
back with the reaction that circulation would be 'most unhelpful'. The
offending document was promptly put in Greenwell's safe and was never
circulated to clients.[5]

There were other incidents involving the Bank, one of which was particularly memorable. Pip Greenwell received a telephone call from a non-
executive director of the Bank saying that criticism in the *Bulletin* was
starting to damage the Bank's reputation and suggesting a dinner at which
to mediate. There were four people present. The confrontation was
between me and Christopher Dow, who was the executive director of the
Bank in charge of the Economic Intelligence Department and a truly ven-
erable Keynesian. Pip was my supporting 'friend' and Christopher Dow's
was the non-executive director of the Bank. Mr Dow could not have been
nicer. He tried very hard to translate my analysis into his Keynesian way
of thought. His intellect was such that he succeeded but the translation
was very complicated. Further, the balance of an argument that was often
clear using monetary analysis was far from clear using his type of analysis. Overall there was not much reconciliation.

A remarkable feature about the above story was that the non-executive
director put into bat by the Bank was the vice-chairman of Greenwell's
second most important client. Was the Bank being naive or was there a
hint of blackmail?

On another occasion a *Bulletin* really did upset the Bank. It pointed out
that the Bank had a vested interest in high inflation because its profits rose in
real terms as inflation increased. The reasoning was that the Bank has three
businesses, namely it is banker to the government; it is the central bank (that
is, it is the bankers' bank); and it has some private business. According to its
published accounts the Bank has just two departments, namely the Issue
Department and the Banking Department. The former covers mainly the first
of the three businesses whereas the latter covers the other two and is very
profitable. At the time the *Bulletin* was written, the Bank liked to give the
impression that a substantial portion of the Banking Department's profits
came from its private business. This allowed it to claim that it was not part
of the public sector and was not subject to controls on public expenditure,
particularly on public sector pay. The result was that salaries in the Bank
tended to be higher than those in the Treasury.[6]

The true position was that the majority of the Banking Department's
profits came from the central-banking business. At the time the mandatory
deposit that a clearing bank had to keep with the Bank was 2 per cent of its
eligible liabilities, which was much larger than under the current regulations.

The total amount of these bankers' deposits was substantial. The Bank did not pay interest on them but earned interest itself when the money was invested in treasury bills, etc. These earnings accounted for a large part of the Bank's profits.

The earnings and, therefore, the Bank's profits rose faster than inflation because of a combination of two factors. First, any rise in inflation is preceded by an increase in the money supply; mandatory deposits rise in line; and so does the amount of interest earned on them. Second, the Bank's earnings depend on the level of interest rates, which also rises with inflation. Hence the assertion in the *Bulletin* that the Bank had a vested interest in high inflation.[7] Publication of this analysis was not welcomed. For clarification, the *Bulletin* did not mean to suggest that officials of the Bank were deliberately giving priority to their institution's vested interest but that such a vested interest was wrong in principle.

3 Fly on the Wall during the Thatcher Revolution

The *Monetary Bulletin* first came to the attention of a senior politician in the early 1970s when the Conservatives were in power. I had been aware that Charles Goodhart was making a précis of them for the Governor of the Bank but not that they were being passed on to the Chancellor of the Exchequer.[1] I was very surprised to learn a year or so later from Anthony Barber (now Lord Barber) that he had even seen some of the drafts. As explained in the previous chapter the Bank had been kept closely in touch whilst analysis was being developed, and this included sending Charles an early draft. I was perturbed to learn that some of drafts had found their way to the Chancellor, as the final version often bore little resemblance to the first draft. (Later on I unintentionally got my own back on Charles, as described below.)

3.1 A BOW GROUP MEETING

The Conservatives lost power in February 1974. A month later the Bow Group held its annual seminar at Magdalen College, Oxford and this turned into a post-mortem. One of Greenwell's partners, Peter Lilley, was the current chairman of the Group and he asked me to give one of the lectures.[2] I chose the title 'An Economic Threat to Democracy'. The pre-pared lecture was extremely critical of the policy that had been followed by the Heath government, including the Prices and Incomes Policy. I was apprehensive when I saw Sir Geoffrey Howe (now Lord Howe) in the front row of the audience, as he had been the 'Minister for Prices', but it was too late to chicken and I decided that I might as well call a spade a bloody shovel (see Howe 1994: 70–1, 75–6).

The upshot was that Geoffrey introduced me to Sir Keith Joseph (the late Lord Joseph) and Robert Carr (now Lord Carr), the latter being the shadow chancellor. In November Margaret Thatcher became Robert Carr's assistant spokesman on Treasury matters and I soon met her. She was in our office whilst we were writing the *Bulletin* that commented on Denis Healey's November 1974 budget, which was an early example of use of analysis of sectoral flow of funds to predict financial pressure on industry and to forecast a deepening recession.

3.2   THE LABOUR GOVERNMENT

In January 1975 I was invited to dinner at 10 Downing Street by the Prime Minister. Immediately after Harold Wilson (the late Lord Wilson) had received his guests the Governor of the Bank, Gordon Richardson (now Lord Richardson), took me on one side and explained that a series of dinners had been agreed when Labour were in opposition; the Prime Minister was the host; he, the Governor, was responsible for the guest list; and he thought that it would a good idea for the Prime Minister to be exposed to the sort of thing I was writing in the *Bulletin*. We were called to dinner before the Governor could elaborate. After the meal was over the Prime Minister explained the occasion and asked his guests to express their concerns. The response was silence. He tried again and the same thing happened. The Governor then tried and there was again silence. He then mentioned some of the subjects he thought were causing concern in the City and looked at me. I was easily the youngest and most junior in the room. I gulped and decided to speak up about monetary growth, the PSBR and public expenditure, whereupon all hell broke loose as far as I was concerned. Harold Wilson appeared to be allergic to having a monetary economist at his dinner table and I was lambasted. Trying to argue with a well-briefed Prime Minister is daunting but I attempted to stand my ground. It went on and on. Michael Marriot, the current chairman of The Stock Exchange, who died tragically shortly afterwards, tried to rescue me but was carved up. Eventually, after what seemed ages, Jeremy Morse (ex-Bank and the then current chairman of Lloyds Bank) chipped in; I will always be grateful to him.

I first met Denis Healey on the day of a Christmas lunch of the Stock Exchange's council at which he was the guest of honour. The lunch, to which I was not invited, happened to coincide with publication of data for the money supply and I was having difficulty writing a *Bulletin*. I was interrupted four times, each time for the same reason, and I lost my temper on the fourth occasion. The reason was 'Had I heard that the Chancellor had said "the City should learn to take Pepper with a pinch of salt"?' A couple of hours later I was at a reception at the US ambassador's residence. After the tensions of the day I was relaxing over a gin and tonic when the US Treasury representative in London brought the Chancellor into the room and introduced him to the people immediately behind me.

I found myself back-to-back with the Chancellor and I suddenly heard myself whisper in his ear 'Mr Salt, Sir'. Mr Healey whirled round, put his arm round my shoulders and chatted for quite a while, much to the chagrin of the people to whom he had just been introduced.[3] (He thought his joke was original; anyone with the surname Pepper knows that it is *not!*)

3.3   MRS THATCHER

Reverting to the Conservatives – Mrs Thatcher became Leader of the Party in February 1975 and organised a number of occasions when financiers and economists met with senior figures in the shadow cabinet to discuss future policy. The outsiders subsequently dropped out one by one until only Samuel Brittan (now Sir Samuel) and I were left.

The Tory Party then appeared to turn inwards. I presumed that the stage was over at which ideas were considered; that basic policy had been formulated; and that detailed work on the manifesto had started. I appeared to be one of the few outside economists still in touch. I used to spend a couple of hours or so with Mrs Thatcher just before a budget and prior to a Conservative Party conference. In some ways I filled in for Alan Walters whilst he was in Washington between 1975 and 1980 (see Thatcher 1995: 303).

During my sessions with Mrs Thatcher I may have been partly responsible for her subsequent hostility towards both clearing banks and the Bank. Regarding the former, I explained how the Ford Motor company was often the pace-setter for manual workers' pay; that the clearing banks were often the pace-setter for clerical workers' pay; and how the latter fed through to the civil service. I explained how a monetary squeeze put financial pressure on industry and market forces then worked to reduce manual workers' wage settlements, but that the opposite happened with the clearing banks. At the time I was briefing Mrs Thatcher the clearing banks did not pay depositors any interest on current accounts but they themselves earned interest on the money deposited with them and, as a result, made a profit. These profits rose as interest rates increased, which happened during a monetary squeeze. With higher profits the clearing banks could afford higher wages. The result was that market forces worked in the wrong direction in the short run. An excellent example of clearing banks conceding excessive wage claims occurred shortly after my conversation with Mrs Thatcher.

My criticism of the Bank was more basic. In my opinion there is something fundamentally wrong with the Bank's mode of operation. The Bank was partly responsible for the awful inflation following the Heath–Barber boom. The cause was not merely promiscuous fiscal policy and that Mr Heath (now Sir Edward) would not allow interest rates to rise. *Competition and Credit Control* removed controls and released a reservoir of money and credit that the Bank completely failed to control. In my view the Bank bears a share of the blame. (The same applies to the Lawson boom; the Bank failed to control a credit explosion that was more important than the more commonly blamed tax cuts.) The Bank also dragged its feet over the introduction of monetary targets and later over the Medium Term Financial Strategy.

I had also been impressed by a paper by John Greenwood, of GT Management in Hongkong and editor of the *Asian Monetary Monitor*, analysing how Pacific basin countries had coped with the rise in inflation following the increase in the price of oil in 1973. He divided the countries into those with central banks modelled on the Bank of England and others. The former fared worse.

The result is that I developed a love-hate relationship with the Bank. Some of the professionalism in the Bank is marvellous and I greatly respect the intellect and integrity of its officials. Nevertheless I came to the conclusion that the culture of the Bank was one of the reasons for English sickness, or British disease as the Americans call it. As well as exporting bloody-minded trade unions to Australia we exported flawed central banking.[4]

3.4   MONETARY BASE CONTROL

More specifically I argued that the Bank's method of trying to hit a monetary target was flawed. The Bank operates on the demand for money rather than on its supply. It tries to predict the demand for money from its forecasts of the economy. It then calculates the level of interest rates that will bring the demand for money into line with the target for the money supply, the intention being to alter interest rates accordingly. Many things can go wrong with this demand-side process. The alternative is for the Bank to operate directly on supply. Technically this method is called monetary base control (MBC). (See Pepper 1990b: 13, 51–54, 58–69 and 1990a.) Shortly after she became Prime Minister in May 1979 Mrs Thatcher commissioned an enquiry into MBC.[5] The decision was unfortunately not to introduce it. (See Howe 1994: 152; Lawson 1992: 79–80, 452; and also Pepper 1993.)

This brings me to how I inadvertently got my own back on Charles Goodhart. During one of my visits to 10 Downing Street I told

Mrs Thatcher that a draft of the Bank's submission to the enquiry about MBC was in existence. When one sees the Prime Minister an official is always present to take notes and to follow up anything material that transpires. I was told later that the Treasury representative in Number 10 sent a memo to the Chancellor asking for a copy of the draft. Geoffrey Howe denied its existence but he covered his back by passing on the request to the Governor who gave the same reply. Meanwhile I had been given a copy for comment and was unwise enough to send it to Mrs Thatcher. My conduct did not exactly make friends in high places. This illustrates how dangerous it can be to talk to a Prime Minister. I subsequently tried to make sure that I did not cross wires with official lines of communication. The solution was to talk instead to Alan Walters. After he returned to London we kept closely in touch.

I asked to see the Governor of the Bank only once. Shortly after he was appointed in 1983 Robin Leigh-Pemberton (now Lord Kingsdown) agreed to a meeting. A few months earlier, just before the tenth anniversary of the start of the *Bulletin*, we had produced a special one entitled 'Improving Practical Monetarism' in which we had expressed our fears that financial innovation would make interpretation of the monetary aggregates ridiculously complicated. We predicted confusion and expressed the concern that the current approach would become so complicated that it would break down in practice. I suggested to the Governor that it would be wise to return to basics at a time of rapid change. Monetarism is about maintaining financial discipline. Control of the money supply implies control of bank deposits. This implies limits on the growth of the banking sector's balance sheet. The growth of the Bank's own balance sheet is even more basic. I told the Governor that monetary policy would not be based on a firm foundation until the Bank limited the growth of its own balance sheet. I accused the Bank of being keen to impose discipline on others but of being very reluctant to accept discipline itself. (This argument was in fact another way of advocating MBC.) I left with the impression that I had not made myself understood.

3.5   GEOFFREY HOWE

I also had direct contact with the Chancellor. Geoffrey Howe organised some seminars at the Treasury at which I was included (see Howe 1994: 113). The one when the Medium Term Financial Strategy was being considered was particularly memorable. I argued for the strategy to include only the variables that were under, or should be under, the authorities' control, for example the money supply and public expenditure. The PSBR is not under a government's control, because it alters according to the phase of the business cycle, rising in a recession and falling in a boom, and no government has found a way to prevent booms and recessions. I argued that the PSBR should be adjusted for the business cycle, that is, it should be expressed on a constant-employment basis in spite of the difficulties surrounding such a calculation. My argument was not accepted. It was thought that a constant-employment PSBR would be too complicated for public consumption and that the strategy would not be credible without inclusion of the PSBR itself. This was an example of how harm can come from concentrating on presentation rather than on policy (see Chapter 4). Even in 1996 people still do not seem to realise the way in which a rise in the PSBR in a recession is offset by a fall in bank lending to the private sector and how in a boom the automatic fall in the PSBR is needed to compensate for a rise in bank lending. The PSBR should be allowed to act as one of the economy's self-stabilisers.

3.6   NIGEL LAWSON

Nigel Lawson subsequently succeeded Geoffrey Howe as Chancellor. He was appointed after the Conservatives were elected for a second term of office in June 1983. During that summer he carried out a detailed review of policy and this included Monetary Base Control. I had two long sessions with him. His conclusion was apparent from the second. He explained that if we changed to MBC then there was no option but for the Bank to be in charge of the transitional arrangements; that the Bank was still 'implacably hostile' to MBC; and that the chance of a body so hostile implementing it successfully was slim. In short the risk/reward ratio was wrong (see Lawson 1992: 80–1, 452, 853).

Nigel Lawson also held regular meetings with a group of outside independent economists (the 'Gooies') (see ibid.: 389–90, 718, 805, 806, 847). Unfortunately I was not invited to attend until January 1988, after the Wall Street crash, and so the warning of inflation sounded in our August 1987 *Bulletin* (see Section A.9.1.9, p. 151) was missed. I was asked to be the lead speaker at my first meeting and gave an early warning of debt-deflation. Nigel Lawson's account is as follows:

> I vividly recall Pepper warning in stark tones that we were faced with the imminent danger of world recession or worse, brought about by an economy that had become far too 'loaned up' (that, or something very

like it, was the unusual expression he used); as a result of which debt deflation stared us in the face. In one sense Pepper was very perceptive and ahead of the game; but because he got the timing so wrong, to have acted on his analysis would have been very much worse than anything I did do. The moral is that it is no use being right too soon. (Lawson 1992: 390)

Gordon Pepper's warning ... of the imminence of a severe recession – indeed he excused himself for leaving early to give a talk on that very subject. The danger to the financial system which so alarmed him was not mythical. He simply got his timing wrong and was ahead of the game. (Ibid.: 806)

I plead guilty to being too early. The subject of debt deflation was new to me too and it took a little while to put it into perspective. The warning was soon qualified; see Section A.9.1.12, pp. 154–6. Nigel's comments do however illustrate a dilemma. The aim should be to give a warning sufficiently early for remedial action to be taken, but it can take some nine months before fiscal policy affects the economy and the time lag between excessive monetary growth and the subsequent rise in inflation can be as long as two years. The result is that a timely warning may have to be sounded many months in advance of an expected event. It is difficult to avoid the accusation of 'crying wolf too soon'.

In *The View from No. 11* Nigel Lawson does not report an argument between us in the middle of 1988. I was most concerned about the buoyant growth of bank lending that was occurring at the time and that was feeding through to excessive growth of M3/M4. The result was a financial bubble in asset prices, including house prices. Nigel was not concerned because it was a private sector phenomenon. If M3/M4 had been growing because of action by the public sector, for example a high PSBR, he would have acted, but because the explanation was action by the private sector his policy was one of benign neglect. My response was that it might not be appropriate for the Treasury to interfere with market forces and individual choice, but preventing excessive growth of credit certainly came within the sphere of responsibility of a central bank and 'he should go away and read some central banking history'. (The last remark was probably not appreciated, but then Nigel liked robust argument!) Our August 1988 *Bulletin* elaborated on the theme; it is reproduced as Appendix 3.1.

In general I found the other meetings of the Gooies of little use, as they were dominated by Samuel Brittan arguing in favour of the Exchange Rate Mechanism of the European Monetary System (ERM) and Patrick

Minford taking the opposite view. This subject was of course most important but Samuel's and Patrick's opinions were well enough known not to need restatement (see Lawson 1992: 390).

3.7 THE ADVENT OF THATCHERISM

Some remarks about the advent of Thatcherism may be appropriate. Firstly there is the general point that the origination of an idea does not mean that it will be adopted, however good it is. Ideas can be left on the 'shelf' for a long time. An interesting question is why implementation occurs when it does. One explanation, for example, can be the arrival of a powerful lobby of vested interests in favour of implementation. This does not appear to have been the case in the late 1970s.

3.8 THE SIGHT OF AN ABYSS

The driving force behind change was the UK arriving in the mid-1970s at the brink of an economic abyss. Senior officials and politicians had sight of the abyss. They were shocked and frightened.

I remember an evening function that was attended by all the main forecasting bodies, namely, the Treasury, the Bank, the National Institute of Economic and Social Research, the London Business School, Wynne Godley from the Department of Applied Economics at Cambridge (representing the New Cambridge School) and so on. They were all having a similar difficulty. Their models would only forecast an acceptable outcome for the economy, in terms of unemployment, inflation and the balance of payments, if the assumptions were unrealistically favourable. There was general agreement that the UK, which had been declining relatively to other OECD countries, was in serious danger of absolute decline and that 'we could not go on like this'.

The Treasury had thought that they could prevent a recession deepening by deploying the Keynesian remedy of a boost to demand. The public sector borrowing requirement had however risen to over 10 per cent of GDP, which was far higher than any Keynesian in the 1950s or 1960s had envisaged.[6] At this level of deficit the perception was that a further increase would not work and might be counterproductive because of the probable adverse reaction of financial markets. The Neo-Keynesians in the Treasury felt naked.

There was a distinction between the reaction of those who were in London and learnt the lesson for themselves and those who learnt it second-hand. One senior Treasury official, who was posted abroad at the time, appeared later to have learnt little, possibly because he had been interpreting things as favourably as he could when briefing foreigners about events in the UK.[7]

The situation can be summed up colloquially. Things often have to get worse before people will accept change and they can get better. By the second half of the 1970s things had got sufficiently worse and the search for change had begun.

3.9   THE SEARCH FOR CHANGE

Two basic ideas were on the shelf, namely, a siege economy and free markets, the latter including control of the money supply as advocated by Milton Friedman (see Friedman 1960, 1968, and Friedman and Schwartz, 1963).

Radical thinking is more likely to come from the political party in opposition than the one in power. If Labour had been in opposition rather than the Conservatives the siege-economy option would probably have been chosen. It would have involved the introduction of the sort of controls to which the UK has only been subject in time of war. The idea was that structural changes to the economy could be forced through under the discipline of such controls.[8] The policy would not have worked and the situation would have deteriorated even further. The Conservatives would eventually have been returned to power and would then have followed the policy that they in fact adopted in the late 1970s.

The policy adopted by the Conservatives was a combination of the theories developed by Milton Friedman and Hayek (see Hayek 1976), which can be divided into measures that affect the financial economy and those that affect the real economy. The financial measures involved gradually reducing monetary growth. The real ones included a whole host of supply-side measures. My own expertise is about the financial economy and I will concentrate on this.

3.10   FINANCIAL DISRUPTION

The financial part of the policy, as I saw it, was not merely to reduce inflation. In the 1970s the UK's financial system had been badly out of equilibrium. Both the budget deficit and balance of payments deficit had grown out of control and there had been a credit explosion. The result had been grossly excessive monetary growth and domestic credit expansion (DCE). Inflation, interest rates and the exchange rate had fluctuated wildly, and there had been crises in the foreign exchange market and stockmarkets that had forced governments to change policy. This financial instability had severely disrupted industry. Near chaos in the 'financial economy' had greatly hindered the 'real economy'.

The objective of monetary policy was, as I saw it, to restore the financial system to approximate equilibrium and to stop it being disruptive. Much of industry's criticism of the City was correct but the proposals from the various inquiries into the financing of industry (for example the Wilson Committee) had been tinkering with symptoms rather than tackling the problem at its roots. Restoring the financial system to equilibrium was an essential prerequisite to solving the problems of the real economy, the latter being a much harder task.

3.11 GRADUALISM

There were two ways of restoring the financial system to equilibrium; it could be done either gradually or by shock treatment. Under the former, targets for the money supply would be announced and would be reduced each year to put sustained downward pressure on inflation. Advocates of this policy argued against inadequate, as well as excessive, monetary growth. The planned reductions in monetary growth would inevitably entail some recessionary pressure.[9] Monetary growth below target would increase this pressure and lead to an unnecessarily deep recession that might get out of control.

3.12 TWO-TERM POLICY

The great disadvantage of the gradualist approach was that reducing inflation in this way would be a long-drawn-out process. There were serious doubts about whether the electorate would be sufficiently patient to allow the policy to run its course. *It was a policy that would require at least two terms of office. There was a grave danger that a government following such a policy would be thrown out of office at the end of its first term of office, in which case the incoming government would almost certainly execute a massive U-turn and the end-result would be appalling.* Mrs Thatcher's response to this argument was that getting re-elected for a second term of office was a political and not an economic matter and to leave it to her.

The danger of not being re-elected might have been avoided if shock treatment had been chosen rather than gradualism. With shock treatment it might have been possible to reduce inflationary expectations very quickly and, after this had been done, economic growth could be resumed.

Under the alternative policy the shock would have been short and very sharp. As far as the sharpness is concerned, the shock should have been large enough to ensure that inflationary expectations were broken completely. As far as shortness is concerned, the shock should have been very brief, so as to minimise the risk of chain reactions and bankruptcies. Such a policy would nevertheless have run the risk of inducing a financial crash. It was inevitable that it was not chosen because politicians and officials were not prepared to take responsibility for such a dangerous policy.[10] The decision was to adopt the gradualist approach to control of the money supply.

3.13　MRS THATCHER AND MONETARISM

I am often asked whether Mrs Thatcher was a monetarist. I cannot give a definite answer but I can shed some light on the subject. Firstly Mrs Thatcher hated inflation. Inflation erodes the real value of people's hard-earned savings and she thought this immoral. Secondly she accepted the *general* proposition that excessive monetary growth in due course leads to a rise in inflation. Because she accepted this she attached great importance to preventing excessive monetary growth and, in this sense, was a monetarist. This does not mean that she accepted the detail of monetary analysis.

As far as detail is concerned I do not remember ever having discussed the relative merits of narrow and broad money or describing the distortions that can occur (as described in Chapter 11). Nevertheless I find it inconceivable that Mrs Thatcher did not delve into the detail. I can give an example about her insistence on doing so. On one occasion when I was summoned to Number Ten Mrs Thatcher had just returned from a gruelling quick trip to the Far East, so much so that she was obviously suffering from jet-lag. We discussed Monetary Base Control. She started to enquire about esoteric detail and I suggested that she should not bother as she had more important things to do. Her response was a very straight back – she was sitting – and an assertion that she could not possibly go into court as a barrister and do justice to her client if she had not mastered all the detail of her brief. Because of her insistence on detail she became renowned as the best briefed person at meetings. Others may have thought they were briefing her but she was often ahead of them.

In 1980 Sir Alfred Sherman, the co-founder of the Centre for Policy Studies, commissioned a paper about the UK monetary situation that was written by Jürg Niehens (Niehens 1981). Mrs Thatcher saw it and it would have been completely out of character for her not to have delved into the detail it contained.

The other side of Mrs Thatcher was that she hated high interest rates because of their effect on the housing market and her vision of a property-owning democracy. Her reluctance to raise interest rates was well known and this gave many people the impression that she gave higher priority to keeping rates down than to control of the money supply. The fact is that she was well aware that lower inflation was the key to reducing interest rates and that interest rates could not be held down for long if inflation was not controlled. The clash between control of the money supply and low interest rates only occurs in the short run; there is no clash over the long term. Mrs Thatcher accepted that control of the money supply was essential if interest rates were to be permanently reduced.

Her reputation for hostility to any suggestion that interest rates should be raised was reinforced by her being almost allergic to some of the arguments advanced for a rise. For example, when the Governor of the Bank and the Chancellor of the Exchequer went round to Number Ten to argue for a rise, the main argument deployed by the Governor was that there would be a collapse in confidence in either the foreign exchange or the discount market, or both, if the Prime Minister did not agree to a rise. The argument was expressed in this way because the Bank considered that it was up to the Treasury to advance the economic arguments and that its particular expertise was its first-hand knowledge of markets. Mrs Thatcher had little confidence in the Bank's reading of market psychology and the result was that the Governor sometimes got a roasting.

I probably contributed to one such event. In January 1983 interest rates were raised while Mrs Thatcher was touring the Falklands Islands. On her return home the Governor had an appointment with her in the afternoon and, presumably, thought that it was to brief her about the reason for the rise. I had however seen her in the morning and had told her that the rise had been unnecessary as monetary growth was under control and that the authorities had caved into to pressure from the money and foreign exchange markets. I also explained how people with vested interests 'talked their book'; that is, if they would profit from a rise in rates they would spread rumours and brief the press in a way that made a rise more likely. The case I advanced to Mrs Thatcher was based on *Bulletin* no. 139, January 1983, which is reproduced in Appendix 3.2. The result of my meeting with the Mrs Thatcher was that the Governor did not find a

Prime Minister waiting to be briefed but rather himself 'on the mat' being ticked off. This and other such occasions lead to the impression that the Prime Minister attached more importance to keeping interest rates down than to monetary control. Alan Walters reports, in contrast, that, although Mrs Thatcher would insist on him justifying his case, she would concede whenever he argued that a rise in interest rates was needed to control the money supply and prevent inflation from rising over the longer term.

APPENDIX 3.1   EXTRACT FROM *MONETARY BULLETIN*, NO. 199, AUGUST 1988

If the public sector is seen to be the cause of an economic problem, the Government acts. If the problem is seen to come from the private sector, the Government tends to wash its hands of it, arguing that it is wrong to interfere with market forces and individual choice.

One example of the above tendency is the Government's attitude to the large deficit which is materialising on the current account of the balance of payments. If the deficit were a reflection of a high budget deficit, as is the case in the US, the Government would act. Because it is a reflection of the behaviour of the private sector, the Government's policy is one of benign neglect ... whilst the deficit is being financed by a capital inflow.

Another example concerns liquidity, more precisely the broader definitions of the money such as M3 and M4. If the current growth of liquidity were a reflection of the behaviour of the pubic sector, the Government would act. If it were due to a rise in the PSBR, sales of gilt-edged stock to the non-bank private sector would be increased ... Currently the Government is not increasing its sales of gilt-edged stock to offset the buoyancy of liquidity because it is a reflection of the behaviour of the private sector, more precisely because it is due to buoyant bank lending to the private sector ...

The reason for the Government's bias is the belief that interference with market forces and individual choice usually does more harm than good. Post war attempts to fine tune the level of demand in the economy through fiscal policy probably increased the volatility of GDP rather than reduced it. The preference not to fine tune also extends to the money supply. Monetarists argue that the authorities should not follow a policy of deliberately varying monetary growth to counteract fluctuations in business activity; our knowledge is inadequate for such a policy to be successful and the best course of action is to ensure steady monetary growth.

The Government's argument that intervention with market forces and individual choice is undesirable is one thing but to argue that the private sector of the economy is inherently stable is another ... The private sector may not in fact be stable. In the days before Keynes invented fiscal policy and before the public sector began to grow, there was a history of financial crises and collapses. Stopping this from happening was a very important reason for the founding of central banks.

The reply to this criticism will probably be that the Bank has a large department responsible for the prudential control of banks ... The focus is, however, on supervision of individual institutions, i.e. on micro-supervision. This misses the whole point because the danger is to the system as a whole, i.e. it is a macro-problem.

It is instructive to ponder why the authorities often rescue a financial institution whilst a larger and more important industrial company, with a much larger workforce, is allowed to go to the wall. The clear impression is one rule for the City and another for industry. The basic rationale why financial institutions are given such special treatment is to prevent a serious chain reaction. With any bankruptcy there is a chance that default will cause someone else to go bankrupt. This danger is far more acute in the financial sector than it is in industry. An important reason for this vulnerability of financial institutions is that their liabilities are normally much higher in relation to their capital than they are for an industrial company. The default of one financial institution can therefore easily start an uncontrollable chain reaction with one following after another ...

The difference between the failure of a financial institution and that of an industrial company suggests very strongly that *prevention of chain reactions should have total priority in the design of prudential control for financial institutions.* The avoidance of chain reaction depends on the health of the financial sector as a whole and is, by definition, a macro-problem.

The prudential supervisors in the Bank concentrate, in contrast, on preventing an individual financial institution from defaulting. This micro-approach is misguided. The experience of the early 1970s provided substantial evidence to support this assertion. Mr Heath's Government came to power intending to 'allow lame ducks to go to the wall'. The neglect (and ignorance) of macro matters was such that the outcome of the policy was that even a fringe bank like London and County (without a full banking license) could not be allowed to go to the wall because of the risk that the chain reaction could not be controlled.

Macro supervision of the banking sector implies control of the quantity of resources available to the banking sector as a whole. As far as the micro

supervisor is concerned the greater the availability of reserves to an individual bank, the greater the availability of liquidity, the greater the availability of capital to the bank, the more he sleeps peacefully in his bed at
night because such an abundant supply of resources strengthens the position of an individual bank. The macro supervisor, in contrast, has night-
mares. Banks are in business to use their resources to the maximum. Given
both an abundance of overall resources and confidence to make use of
them, banks' balance sheets will expand very rapidly. This will in due
course cause a speculative bubble to be formed. The bubble will inevitably
break at some time in the future, but in a way which cannot be forecast,
both with regard to manner and time. There is, accordingly, a direct clash
between what comforts the micro supervisor and what comforts the macro
supervisor.

The Crash

The crash of equity markets last October [1987] provides a classic example
of what can happen ... The extraordinary event was not October's fall in
markets but the preceding rise. A bull market in ordinary shares normally
occurs as the trough of a recession approaches. At this stage of the business cycle savings normally rise relative to the demand for finance and,
therefore, the underlying financial forces are favourable for capital
markets. Expectations also improve as investors start seeing through the
recession and anticipate an economic upswing, recovery in profit margins,
etc. This was happening in 1986 but, in addition, the Fed in the US and the
Bank in the UK both allowed credit and liquidity to explode. This provided abundant finance for speculation. It was like pouring petrol on a
bonfire. The Bank and the Fed neglected one of the basic duties of a
central bank and must bear prime responsibility for the crash in markets in
October and the acute risk of financial crisis during the aftermath.

APPENDIX 3.2   EXTRACT FROM *MONETARY BULLETIN*,
NO. 139, JANUARY 1983

> *In the foreign exchange market, the authorities' tentative interventions
> have brought them the worst of both worlds and have prolonged the
> period of sterling's adjustment to its previous over valuation.*

> *In domestic markets, too, the authorities have not been decisive. They
> are in danger of aborting the economic recovery by not responding*

appropriately to new pressures posed by the clearing banks. The authorities should concentrate on fundamentals and relate interest rates neither to the exchange rate nor to defects in their arrangements for controlling the banks but to domestic monetary growth, which continues at a satisfactory pace.

The Government's publicly declared policy is not to resist market forces. In practice, their actions are a most important background determinant of those forces. Further, when markets start to move, the Bank of England's reflex action is to intervene directly to 'preserve orderly markets'.

As far as the foreign exchange market is concerned, there are valid reasons for the recent fall in sterling. The reflex action by the authorities to support sterling has resulted in the worst of both worlds. The use of the reserves is a two-edged weapon; the more they are used in the early stages of a major adjustment the greater is the expectation of a one way bet against the currency and of their deployment being discontinued. In the absence of both the commitment and the resources to be successful, the authorities would have been wiser not to have intervened. They should have allowed sterling to fall and to have made it crystal clear that they would subsequently heavily penalise those taking a bear position by encouraging the rate to bounce up again once it had touched bottom. In the event, we have lost reserves and the authorities have prolonged the period of adjustment and uncertainty.

Turning to interest rates, the cause of the recent rise has, of course, been the run on sterling. It is not, however, clear to what extent that rise is the result of deliberate action by the authorities or of their bowing reluctantly to market forces. In our view, the authorities should not be using higher interest rates in an attempt to stop the fall in sterling. Raising interest rates by 1 or 2 per cent is no longer credible in circumstances in which foreign exchange speculators can lose that much per day by being in the wrong currency. The authorities may, instead, have reacted either to the previous acceleration in monetary growth or to what they felt were the imperatives of market forces. As far as the latter is concerned, there is a new and, at the present, very important feature in the market. The clearing banks are now much more eager to raise their base rates than they were in similar circumstances in the past. This development is worth exploring in detail because it has been highly influential in the last few weeks and, after the events of the last few days, continues to be very significant. Without a change in the authorities' responses to it, the pressure for a further rise in interest rates looks set to continue.

Profitability of Clearing Banks

When sterling was weak in the 1970s, nominal interest rates were very high and the banks made large profits out of investing money received from non-interest-bearing deposits in interest-bearing assets. Occasionally the overall level of bank profits became embarrassingly high as a result of this endowment element and the banks tended to take a relaxed attitude to unprofitable marginal business which was expected to be relatively short-lived. They were, in general, receptive to requests from the Bank not to raise rates and, in particular, did not raise their base rates quickly to prevent round-tripping transactions (customers drawing down overdrafts in order to deposit money, usually with another bank, at a higher rate of interest than the overdraft rate).

The current circumstances in which banks are operating are very different. First, the endowment element in banks' profits has been drastically reduced as both interest rates and the proportion of current accounts to total deposits has fallen. Secondly provisions for bad debts, both at home and abroad, are exceptionally high for a time when interest rates are low. Thirdly, administrative costs have not been satisfactorily curtailed. The clearing banks have, accordingly, become very sensitive about any unprofitable lines of business.

Their particular cause for concern is the profitability of loans on which the interest charged is related to base rate (e.g. overdrafts) and which are financed from money raised in the wholesale deposit markets. The proportion of such business has increased substantially over the last year. A year ago the lending by London Clearing Banks to the inter-bank market was £3500m greater than their deposits from it; currently they are roughly in balance. Looking at an individual bank, the proportion of Barclays' deposits tied to market rates has probably risen from under 30 per cent in the first half of 1981 to over 40 per cent in the second half of 1982.

The best measure of the average cost of these market funds is usually the three month LIBOR. As well as paying this rate of interest, banks incur costs which amount to roughly $^3/_4$ per cent for prime borrowers. This covers the provision for liquidity and capital, administrative expenses and reserves against bad debts. The total cost of providing these funds must be compared with the return on them. Prime borrowers in the private sector are charged 1 per cent over base rate. The overall arithmetic is that this type of business starts to become unprofitable when the three month LIBOR rises to a level which exceeds base rates by $^1/_4$ per cent ... [When LIBOR rises above this level] the pressures increase on banks to raise base rates because a substantial amount of business is becoming unprofitable ... this has been the situation for most of the period since the end of November.

4 Monetarism in the 1980s

A crisis in monetarism occurred early in the 1980s. The authorities had chosen to target broad money, more precisely sterling M3 (which included deposit accounts with banks as well as current accounts but excluded accounts denominated in foreign currency). In 1980–1 the target was missed by a large amount; sterling M3 grew by more than 18 per cent compared with the target of 7 per cent to 11 per cent.[1] Worse still for the reputation of monetarism, the economy was in a recession that was obviously deepening and this suggested that monetary policy should be eased rather than tightened. In the event Geoffrey Howe ignored the behaviour of sterling M3 and reduced base rates. During the following year the target for sterling M3 was again overshot. Nigel Lawson subsequently introduced a target for M0 (the narrowest of the monetary aggregates) and switched between sterling M3 and M0. Later on, he abandoned monetary control and focused instead on sterling's exchange rate.

The result of the above was a widespread public impression that monetarism had been tried in the 1980s, found wanting and failed. It may seem surprising but this impression is wrong. The main explanation of the apparent failure was that the monetary aggregates had become distorted and allowance should have been made for this. The distortions are described below, but first it should be appreciated that there were two distinct reasons for adopting monetary targets. One was control of the money supply for its own sake. The other was to manage expectations or, more generally, that the targets could be used for political purposes. The policy was certainly a complete failure as far as the latter was concerned.

4.1 THE POLITICS OF MONEY SUPPLY TARGETS

The original neo-Keynesian argument for setting a monetary target was to try to stop financial markets from enforcing undesirable policy changes on the government (see Wass 1978). The classic example of such an incident was the sterling crisis in the autumn of 1976, when Chancellor Healey had to turn back from London airport and the UK had subsequently to borrow from the IMF, which involved tightening monetary and fiscal policy. In the 1970s there were also examples of 'buyers' strikes' in the gilt-edged market enforcing a change in policy.

4.1.1 Managing Expectations

At the time explanations were sought for the erratic behaviour of financial markets. According to the efficient-market hypothesis, which has dominated most economists' thinking about financial markets during the last two decades or so, the explanation for a change in the level of a market is unexpected news altering people's expectations. (This view is challenged in Pepper 1994, which argues that flows of funds can be an explanation for the behaviour of a financial market.) Volatile expectations were thought to be the reason for the erratic behaviour of markets and the remedy was to manage expectations. It was argued that the introduction of monetary targets would help to do this, in particular that the targets would reassure financial markets that the government accepted the need for financial discipline and that this would reduce inflationary expectations.

The above is a particular example of a general argument often deployed by neo-Keynesians. If an economic forecast turns out to be wrong, the most common explanation advanced by them is that there has been an unexpected alteration in savings. This is thought, in turn, to be due to a change in 'confidence'. The importance of confidence and changes in it are repeatedly stressed. A typical comment in a recession for example is that everything would be all right if only confidence would return. Hence official attempts to manage confidence. The introduction of monetary targets was an example of the authorities trying to do this.

4.1.2 Curtailing Public Expenditure

Another argument for monetary targets used in the 1980s was that targets for both the money supply and the public sector borrowing requirement (PSBR) would strengthen control of public expenditure. The first stage of the reasoning was that a limit on the PSBR was necessary to control the money supply. The next stage was that strict control of public expenditure was needed if the PSBR was to be limited without taxes having to rise. This argument strengthened the hand of the Treasury ministers when they were arguing with ministers in charge of spending departments. Indeed the author was reprimanded by Mrs Thatcher in the early 1980s for making comments about the money supply undershooting its target; he was told that they were most unhelpful because they destroyed one of the arguments being deployed at the time by the Treasury and weakened the battle to control public expenditure. This was an excellent example of a clash between control of the money supply for its own sake and as a political objective.

Control of the money supply also had particular appeal to the Bank. Whenever inflationary pressures arise the Bank nearly always advocates that fiscal policy should be tightened. If the target for broad money is being, or is in danger of being, overshot, as is usually the case when inflation threatens, the Bank can use the existence of the target as an argument to tighten fiscal policy. The existence of the target helps the Bank to argue its case.

4.1.3 Overcoming Political Resistance

There was also another argument that appealed to some in the Bank. If a discretionary policy is being followed and the Bank judges that a rise in interest rates is appropriate, its political masters may object because the rise will be unpopular with the electorate, in particular amongst people with mortgages and businessmen. The existence of a target for the money supply might help the Bank to argue its case; it might help to overcome political resistance to a rise in rates (the Bank did not in fact use this argument when Mrs Thatcher was Prime Minister; see Section 3.13, p. 31).

Summarising, a central bank can be in favour of setting a target for the money supply even if it is agnostic about monetarism. The Bank's attitude to monetarism and the priority it gave to the politics of money supply targets were in fact described in a speech 'Setting Monetary Objectives' by John Fforde (1983). Mr Fforde was the executive director of the Bank responsible for domestic monetary policy when targets for the money supply were first adopted. His speech stressed the political reasons. Official policy was described as 'more eclectic than monetarist'. It explained that the policy was 'due only in part to its associated and often "monetarist" economics'. The whole tone of the speech suggested that the Bank was in favour of monetary targets primarily for political reasons and not for control of the money supply for its own sake.

The introduction of the Green Paper *Monetary Control* in March 1980 sheds further light on the progression between how the policy was meant to work in practice and how it should be set out in public:[2]

No single statistical measure of the money supply can be expected fully to encapsulate monetary conditions, and so provide a uniquely correct basis for controlling the complex relationships between monetary growth and prices and nominal incomes. The degree of substitutability

between forms of money or liquidity just inside or outside their respect-
ive measures means that it is insufficient to rely on one measure alone:
in assessing monetary conditions the authorities have to have regard to a
range – including not only the narrow measure (M1) but the wider
measures of money (M3, sterling M3) and various still wider measures
of private sector liquidity... (p. iii)

As no one aggregate is by itself a sufficient measure of monetary conditions it could be argued that there should be targets for several or all.
But this would make it much more difficult for the market and the
public to appraise the determination of the authorities to meet their
monetary objectives... (p. iv)

For the present, therefore, the Government intends:–
(a) to formulate the monetary target in relation to one aggregate;
(b) to continue to use sterling M3 for this purpose;
(c) to take into account growth of other aggregates, directing policy to
     progressive and sustained reduction in the rate of growth of all,
     although not necessarily by the same amount. (p. v)

The policy was published in full in the subsequent *Financial Statement
and Budget Report* in March 1980 as part of the first exposition of the
Conservative government's Medium Term Financial Strategy. As planned,
the authorities set a target for only one aggregate but the qualification
about the use of a single aggregate was contained merely in the small print
of a footnote. It must be stressed that the reason for *publishing* monetary
targets was to affect expectations and it was logical to design the exposition to maximise the effect. What was not appreciated at the time was the
way in which this would clash with monetary control for its own sake.

4.1.4   Degree of Precision

An example of the clash between maximising the impact on expectations
and monetary control for its own sake is the desirable degree of precision
at which to aim. The effect on expectations would be maximised if the
targets could be hit precisely. Politicians and officials would also be
pleased with such an outcome as they would avoid criticism. Precision
would however be most undesirable because it would prevent money from
fulfilling one of its basic functions. Money bridges the gap between the
timing of income receipts and expenditure payments. As the timing varies
money balances fluctuate. Stopping the fluctuations would prevent money

from acting as a buffer and a substitute for money would have to be invented. Fluctuations in the money supply that last for six months or less do not affect the economy; it is progressive departures from target that should be prevented and not short-term fluctuations around the target. Precise control of the money supply is not desirable.

4.1.5 Perverse Effect on Expectations

As already stated, sterling M3 hopelessly overshot its targets between 1980 and 1982. The effect of publishing the targets was to raise inflationary expectations rather than lower them. From time to time the overshoot also unsettled the gilt-edged and foreign exchange markets. In the second half of 1980, for example, bond yields were certainly higher than would otherwise have been the case. The effect on expectations was the opposite to that intended. As the policy lost credibility the Government suffered considerable political embarrassment. The opposition parties made the most of it and derided monetarism, with Labour conveniently forgetting that Denis Healey was the first Chancellor of the Exchequer to announce monetary targets.

Summarising, the attempt to manage expectations was a dismal failure. It was a public relations exercise that was not based on reality. As usual with such exercises, it fell flat on its face.

4.2 VESTED INTERESTS

Neo-Keynesians were not the only people to be delighted by the demise of monetarism. Banks were too, and they are a powerful industrial lobby.

It is important to distinguish between bankers and banks. The former, as individuals, are nearly all in favour of 'sound money'. The latter, as corporate bodies, are generally against control of the money supply. The explanation for this apparent inconsistency is vested interest. Monetary control implies a tight constraint on the growth of the balance sheet of the banking sector as a whole. Although one bank can compete with another, the growth of the sector as a whole is strictly limited. Banking would not be a growth industry if the authorities persisted with monetary control.

The clash between banks' ambitions and control of the money supply is illustrated very clearly by what happened between the middle of 1982 and the end of 1988. During this period UK banks *tripled* their sterling assets. This could not have happened if the money supply had been controlled.

There is no doubt that monetary control would have thwarted banks' ambitions. It is no wonder that they argued against it.

4.2.1   Captured Regulators

As stated earlier, the Bank was agnostic to monetarism. As well as being the central bank the Bank is the regulator of UK banks. It is possible that this dual role is an explanation of the Bank's attitude to monetarism. There are many examples in other industries of regulators being captured by the people they are supposed to be regulating (see, for example, Benston 1991). Regulation initially designed to protect consumers often ends up protecting producers. The same may have happened in the banking industry. The Bank's hostility to monetarism may be an echo of the attitude of banks.[3]

The above observation will seem a wild accusation to many in the UK. Perhaps they should ponder on attitudes in Germany where the roles of central bank and banking regulator are split. The Bundesbank argues strongly that the German structure should be adopted in Europe. One of the arguments is that banks tend to suffer when monetary policy is tightened and, if the roles are combined, fears about the health of the banking system can be a reason for a central bank delaying tighter monetary policy. It can be the explanation of 'too little, too late'. The danger of this happening is reduced if the central bank is not the regulator. One of the reasons why the Bundesbank is in favour of monetary control and the Bank is not may be that the former is not responsible for regulating banks whereas the latter is.

4.2.2   Personal Integrity

The accusation may also seem to be an attack on the personal integrity of regulators. It is not. Many regulators are ex-practitioners. Their in-depth knowledge of the industry is extremely valuable. Highly respected people who are the pillars of their profession tend to become regulators towards the end of their careers. They are people of great integrity who are convinced that they are behaving correctly. But they bring with them the mental attitude of their industry.

An extreme example of what can happen is the attitude of the Council of the Stock Exchange in the early 1980s prior to 'Big Bang'. There were valid arguments for and against a change in the structure of the Exchange. Many on the Council focused on the ones in favour of the old structure and convinced themselves that its preservation would be in the national interest. But examine the technology that they were defending. Under the old rules of the Exchange a jobber (that is, a market-maker) was only allowed to make prices by word of mouth to those within earshot. Contrast this with making markets globally over television screens to an unlimited number of people. The old technology was horse-and-cart in an electronic age. It was totally indefensible. But people of integrity had convinced themselves that it should be preserved. This episode illustrates how honour and integrity may not stop regulators from being captured when they have spent most of their working lives absorbing the culture of an industry.

4.3   DISTORTIONS TO DATA

As already stated, distortions to the monetary aggregates were another reason why monetarism fell into disrepute in the 1980s. At times some of the aggregates pointed in one direction whilst others were pointing in the opposite direction. The result was confusion.

Section 2.10 described how the team at Greenwell realised how distortions could cause problems and learnt the remedy early on. Recapitulating, all the aggregates should be monitored and if any of them is behaving in a peculiar way the reasons should be ascertained. The explanation will often involve a change in one interest rate relative to another. The transactions responsible for the change in rates should be investigated, as should those in response to the change. Such an analysis adds greatly to understanding what is happening in the financial system as a whole and it discloses when an aggregate is distorted.

The subject of how to monitor the money supply and the distortions to data that occurred in the 1970s and the 1980s is covered in reasonable depth in a paper by the author, 'Monitoring the Money Supply and Distortions to Monetary Data' given at the 1992 annual conference of the Money, Macro and Finance Research Group, reprinted in the *National Westminster Bank Quarterly Review*, February 1993, and as Chapter 16 of the author's *Money, Credit and Asset Prices* (Pepper 1994).[4] The distortions discussed were known at the time or shortly afterwards and were reported in Greenwell's *Monetary Bulletin*.[5]

If allowance is made for distortions in the way described, experience showed that the aggregates usually gave similar messages. If they did not, the analysis indicated which aggregate was reliable and which was not. On a few occasions all the aggregates were unreliable, in which case it was at least known that the monetary barometer was temporarily jammed and should be disregarded.

4.3.1 Summary

A distinction was made at the start of this chapter between control of the money supply for its own sake and the politics of money supply targets. The problems caused by distortions to the monetary aggregates could usually be overcome if the objective was the former but not if it was the latter, because of the almost inevitable effect of distortions on expectations.

4.4 DISAGREEMENT AMONG MONETARISTS

A final reason for monetarism falling into disrepute was public disagreement amongst monetarists. Whereas there is no doubt that the disagreement contributed to the disrepute in the 1980s, the eventual result may be that monetarism is strengthened because lessons can be learnt from the debate among monetarists, analysis can be tightened, and techniques can be improved. Discussion of this is deferred until Chapter 10.

4.5 A CRUCIAL TEST OF MONETARISM

How then should monetarism in the 1970s and 1980s be judged? It should certainly not be judged in terms of the politics of money supply targets. Monetarism's most important claim is that control of the money supply would control inflation and help to stabilise the real economy. In the event the authorities frequently missed their targets and the money supply, after adjustment for distortions, was not controlled during most of the 1970s and during the second half of the 1980s. Monetarism cannot therefore be judged by the outcome of monetary control.

Given the lack of control, the next strongest test of monetarism is whether departures from target, after allowing for distortions, could be used to predict how economic activity and inflation would vary. Monetarism can be judged on its forecasting record. Were forecasts of growth of GDP and inflation using monetary analysis better or worse than other forecasts, particularly the largely Keynesian ones emanating from macroeconomic models of the economy? (See Pepper 1981: 9–14.)

Part II of this book discusses economic forecasting in general. It assesses the accuracy of predictions and compares the performance of the macroeconomic models with the monetarist method developed at W. Greenwell & Co. It starts with a brief history of macroeconomic modelling.

PART II

The Validity of Monetarism: Economic Forecasts in the 1970s and 1980s

5 A Brief History of Macroeconomic Models[1]

The three main forecasting bodies in the UK are the Centre for Economic Forecasting at the London Business School (LBS), the National Institute for Economic and Social Research (the National Institute or NIESR) and the Treasury (more formally, Her Majesty's Treasury or HMT). All three make use of large macroeconomic models of the economy.

A macroeconomic model is a system of equations and identities that describes the complete economy. (An identity is an equation that is correct by definition.[2]) The models are usually very complicated and have tended to become more so as time has passed. By the end of the 1970s the Treasury's model, for example, had about 600 equations and identities. Electronic computing power is essential to be able to run such a large system.

5.1 FORECASTS BEFORE THE ADVENT OF MODELS

Forecasts of the economy were made well before computer models were developed. Within the public sector the Treasury carried out systematic and regular forecasts. Initially these merely involved establishing trends, extrapolating them, conducting surveys of business expectations and building forecasts around the results.

As time passed the Treasury's forecasting process became more sophisticated. Individual departments of government were given certain assumptions about the possible growth of GDP on which to base their own forecasts of their particular fields of interest. For example those responsible for housing were asked to forecast investment in residential construction, and so on. Elsewhere the balance of payments group prepared forecasts of world trade and exports. These forecasts were then integrated with behavioural equations reflecting consumption and imports to produce second-round estimates of GDP. The process was an iterative one, modified with judgements made at interdepartmental meetings that the Treasury organised and chaired. The final forecast was assembled by the Treasury. It was designed and intended for the government's own use. Forecasts for use by the private sector started in 1959 with the foundation of the *National Institute Quarterly Review*.

5.2   EARLY MODELS

Work on macroeconomic models started in earnest in the UK in the early 1960s. The first regular forecast using such a model was published by the LBS (Ball and Burns) in 1966. The NIESR followed in August 1969. The Treasury, having commissioned Ball and Eaton to describe its existing forecasting system in terms of quantifiable equations, produced the first forecast using its own version of a full-scale model in the summer of 1970. The LBS model subsequently provided the basis from which the Bank began to develop its own model (the Bank's forecasts have never been published). By the early 1970s there were three main forecasting bodies competing with each other; they were the LBS, the NIESR and the Treasury.

5.3   FINANCE

The formation and maintenance of the teams required to sustain serious model-building was expensive. The Ford Foundation provided the initial finance for early work at Cambridge (the Cambridge Growth Project). The Social Sciences Research Council (SSRC) subsequently took over and also provided funds for LBS, NIESR and others. NIESR also obtained finance from the Treasury. In the early 1980s there was a re-examination of the basis for public support of macroeconomic modelling and, following publication of a report by a subcommittee of the SSRC on 'Macroeconomic Research in the United Kingdom', it was decided to finance this activity through a consortium comprising the Bank, the SSRC (renamed the Economic and Social Research Council (ESRC) in 1984) and the Treasury. Funds were provided for four years at a time. The first period was between 1983 and 1986. The second was between 1987 and 1990. Round 3 covered 1991–4 and the current round at the time of writing covers 1995–8. The author was a member of ESRC between 1989 and 1993 (that is, on the council) and chairman of the Macroeconomic Modelling Consortium between 1991 and 1994.

Since the early 1970s public finance has always been provided for LBS and NIESR. Others have come and gone. The Cambridge Economic Growth Project (in its early days a static detailed inter-industry analysis, later on, multi-sectoral dynamic) has already been mentioned. Other examples were Southampton (a very ambitious model in the 1970s), Cambridge Economic Policy Group (Wynne Godley, sectoral flow of funds, 1973–83), City University Business School (Beenstock, supply-side, 1983–7), Liverpool (Minford, rational expectations and supply-side, 1983–90 and 1995–) and Queen Mary College/Imperial College (optimal control methods and control theory, ending in 1990).[3]

5.4 INCORPORATING NEW IDEAS

The LBS and NIESR models were originally Keynesian.[4] LBS later adopted international monetarism (see Frenkel and Johnson, 1976). Both LBS and NIESR have incorporated developments that were made elsewhere, for example their models now include supply-side and rational expectations, and the modelling of labour markets is based on work carried out by the Centre for Labour Economics at LSE under the direction of Richard Layard. LBS and NIESR have also made use of developments in analysis of time series, for example the methods developed by Box and Jenkins, error-correction models and, later, cointegration. Their models have also been fully exposed to control theory. The Treasury's model has evolved in a similar way.

5.5 THE THREE MAIN MODELS

As explained, LBS, NIESR and the Treasury have all three incorporated into their models new developments in economic theory and practice soon after they have materialised. The result is that these models have continued to be the three main ones of the economy. Attention is focused on them in Chapter 8.

6 The Accuracy of Routine Forecasts

Like long-term weather forecasts [economic forecasts] are better than nothing... But their origin lies in the extrapolation from a partially known past, through an unknown present, to an unknowable future according to theories about the causal relationships between certain economic variables which are hotly disputed by academic economists, and may in fact change from country to country and from decade to decade.

Denis Healey (1989: 381)

6.1 MACROECONOMIC MODELS

The simplest and conventional way of assessing the accuracy of a forecast is to compare the prediction of growth of real GDP for the year ahead with the outturn and calculate the error. Such exercises are carried out regularly. NIESR and the Treasury publish their results.

According to the Treasury's 1994 *Financial Statement and Budget Report* (FSBR), for example, during the previous ten years the forecasts for GDP in real terms for the year ahead, published in the *Autumn Statements*, had an average error regardless of sign of $1\frac{1}{2}$ percentage points. One possible explanation for part of this is that before 1993 the *Autumn Statement* did not allow for the policy changes that would be announced in the subsequent budget in March or April (this difficulty no longer arose after 1993 when the budget was moved to the autumn). It may accordingly be fairer to assess the forecasts made in March or April rather than those in the autumn. The 1993 FSBR reported that the average absolute error in these was one percentage point.

The National Institute appears to have had a somewhat similar record if allowance is made for how far in advance a forecast is made. Its *Quarterly Review* in August 1993 gave an assessment of the forecasts it publishes each August. During the previous ten years the average error in the predictions of real GDP for the year ahead was 1.7 per cent, the errors ranging from 0.3 to 4.4 per cent. It is not surprising that these errors were worse than the Treasury's, because the National Institute's forecasts were published in August, three months before the Treasury's, when less information about the run-up to the year in question was available.

6.2   MONETARIST FORECASTS

Monetarists argue that buoyant growth of the money supply always precedes a rise in inflation, and that sluggish monetary growth always precedes a fall in inflation. Being more precise, the sequence of events following buoyant monetary growth is usually a rise in economic activity followed by an increase in inflation. The sequence following sluggish monetary growth is a decline in economic activity and then a fall in inflation. It is however stressed that the time lag between changes in monetary growth and the response of the economy is long and variable.

The variability of the time lag is highly significant. *It means that forecasts of the economy from changes in the money supply, like Keynesian ones, are not accurate.* Both types of forecast are insufficiently accurate to be able to predict the growth of GDP during the year ahead within one percentage point or so.

Monetarists should not dispute the above assertion about inaccuracy. It is in fact central to monetarism. As is well known, monetarists argue that the authorities should aim at predetermined targets for the money supply. One of the reasons for this is that action in a recession to stimulate the economy by boosting monetary growth above the target will lead to an unsustainable recovery if the time lag between monetary growth and the response of the economy is unusually long. Action in a boom to reduce monetary growth below the target range can easily add to the depth of the subsequent recession. Attempts to damp a business cycle, however well meant, can easily amplify it. The fact is that our state of knowledge is insufficient to be able to do so successfully. Anyone who accepts the argument for predetermined targets for the money supply should also accept that monetarist forecasts of the economy are not accurate.

6.3   OTHER FORECASTS

The record of inaccuracy is not confined to large macroeconomic models and monetarists. A paper 'A Comparison of Short-Term Macroeconomic Forecasts' by Andrew Burrell and Stephen Hall of LBS (Burrell and Hall 1993) examines the record of a wide range of forecasters, including academic institutions, commercial organisations and financial institutions.[1] Data from *Economic Forecasts* published monthly since 1984 by North-Holland were scrutinised and the forecasts of GDP a year ahead were shown in various charts. One of the conclusions of the paper was:

> these charts may be interpreted as a damming criticism of economic forecasting. Many years of research effort do not seem to have increased confidence in relatively short-term prediction much beyond simple trend estimation.

6.4   MARKET FAILURE

Why then do economists persist in making routine forecasts of the economy in spite of their techniques being insufficiently accurate? The answer is first that there is a clear demand for the product even if the one delivered is unreliable. Second, any forecaster who wants to be taken seriously has to publish regularly, like it or not, because regular forecasts provide publicity and help to keep the forecaster in the limelight. A forecaster who does not make routine forecasts is excluded from the summary tables of the various forecasts and loses credibility. A third reason is that failure to make regular forecasts has a detrimental effect on the amount of funding that a forecasting team is able to attract.

6.5   CONCLUSION

Forecasts of the growth of GDP during the year ahead are unlikely to be accurate within one percentage point or so whatever method is used. Techniques are insufficiently accurate to be able to predict minor variations in an economic cycle with any confidence. This suggests strongly that forecasters should concentrate instead on trying to predict events that are within the margin of accuracy of their techniques. They should only try to predict major events.

If this line of argument is accepted it follows that monetarism should be judged not on the accuracy of routine forecasts but on its record of predicting major events. Chapter 7 defines major events. Chapter 8 investigates the performance of the three main macroeconomic models and Chapter 9 investigates the record using the approach developed in the Greenwell *Monetary Bulletin*.

7 Major Events

7.1 RECESSIONS

What constitutes a major event? Chart 7.1 illustrates the recessions in the UK since 1968. The graph with the dots shows the coincidental indicators of the economy. The one without dots shows unfilled job vacancies. Four recessions are illustrated:

(i) 1970–1, starting when Roy Jenkins was Chancellor of the Exchequer,

Chart 7.1   Recession – unfilled job vacancies and coincidental indicators, 1969–93

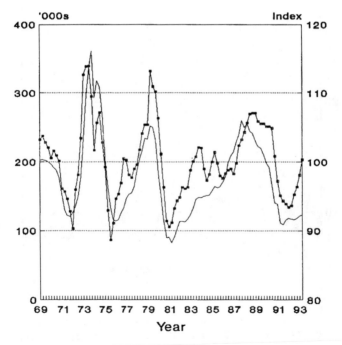

(ii)   1974–5 when Denis Healey was Chancellor,
(iii) 1979–81 when Geoffrey Howe was Chancellor, and
(iv)   1990–2 when Norman Lamont was Chancellor.

There should be no dispute that all of these were major events.

7.2   INFLATIONS

Chart 7.2 shows the behaviour of inflation in the UK since 1968; more precisely, it shows annual changes in the retail price index. There were three periods of rising inflation:

Chart 7.2   Inflations – retail price index, 1969–93

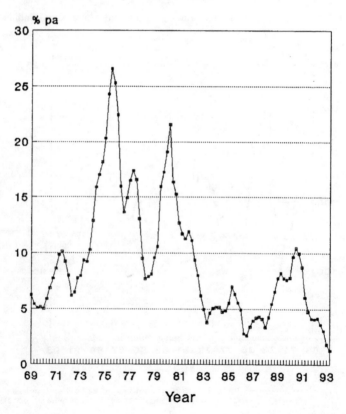

(i)   1973–5 after the Barber boom,
(ii) 1979–80 as a result of the failure to take unpopular measures during the last months of the Labour government (and concealed inflation coming out into the open), and
(iii) 1989–90 after the Lawson boom.

Again it should be agreed that these too were major events.

7.3   FINANCIAL CRISES

There may be less agreement about the next most important events. Some people may assert that deficits in the current account of the balance of payments come next. Others will argue that such deficits do not matter providing that they are financed by an inflow of private capital. Their reasoning is that there will be an inflow of capital from abroad if profitability in a country is abnormally high and that this can lead to a rise in the exchange rate which in turn can be the cause of a deficit on the current account of the balance of payments. If this is the case the current account deficit will be sustainable. Developing countries have financed themselves in such a way over many years.

The event associated with a balance of payments deficit that is important to forecast is a foreign exchange crisis that is sufficiently severe to force a policy change. The IMF crisis in October 1976 is an obvious example. Another is sterling leaving the Exchange Rate Mechanism (ERM) of the European Monetary System (EMS) in October 1992. A difficulty is that predictions of such events are not economic forecasts but forecasts of the behaviour of a financial market which are even more difficult to make.

Crises in other financial markets may also be important events. The crashes in the UK equity market in the autumn of 1973 and in global equity markets in October 1987 are memorable. There have also been the examples of a fall in the gilt-edged market enforcing changes in policy in the UK.

7.4   CONCLUSION

The four recessions and the three inflations identified in this chapter are clearly major events that the forecasting teams should have predicted. They can be judged on how well they did so.

8 The Record of the Large Models

This chapter contains an analysis of how far in advance the London Business School, the National Institute of Economic and Social Research and the Treasury published warnings about the four recessions and the three inflations identified in the last chapter. The first stage of the analysis is to establish when the event in question started; that is, when the recession began or the period of rapid inflation commenced. The second stage is to find out the date on which the earliest warning was given. The dates can then be compared to find out how far in advance the warning was sounded.

8.1 SEQUENCES OF FORECASTS

LBS publishes forecasts four times a year. Its earliest ones are published 38 months prior to the start of the year being forecast. This means that for a particular year there is a sequence of nine forecasts prior to the year's start and three during the year. This sequence can be examined to find out the date of the first warning of an event occurring during the year being forecast.

A similar analysis can be carried out for NIESR. It publishes forecasts four times a year. Its earliest predictions used to be 13 months prior to the start of a year but these were dropped in November 1987 and the lead time since then has been ten months.[1] This means that NIESR now publishes a sequence of four forecasts prior to the start of a year and four during a year.

The Treasury is more cautious. It publishes just two forecasts a year. The earliest one for a calendar year is only about a month prior to the start of the year being forecast. For a particular calendar year the Treasury's sequence is one forecast prior to the year and two during it (but see Section 8.4.2(iii)).

A detailed analysis of the sequences is contained in Appendix 8.1. Two or three adjacent years are examined around each event to give a complete picture of when the warnings were sounded. The conclusions are summarised below.

8.1.1   Summary – Inflations

1973–5	*Date*	*Timing*
Start of rapid rise	3rd quarter 1973	
Peak	3rd quarter 1975	

Predicted:		
NIESR	Aug 1973	At the start of the rapid rise

1979–1980		
Start of rapid rise	4th quarter 1978	
Peak	2nd quarter 1980	

Predicted:		
NIESR	Aug 1979	⎫ Six to eight months
LBS	June 1979	⎬ after the start
Treasury	June 1979	⎭ of the rapid rise

1989–1990		
Start of rapid rise	4th quarter 1988	
Peak	3rd quarter 1990	

Predicted:		
NIESR	May 1989	⎫ Three to six months after
LBS	June 1989	⎬ the start of the rapid rise
Treasury	March 1990	

8.1.2   Summary – Recessions

1970–1		
Downswing	2nd quarter 1969	
Trough	4th quarter 1971	

Predicted:		
NIESR	Aug 1970	Half way through the downswing
Treasury	March 1971	Six months before the trough

1974–5		
Downswing	3rd quarter 1973	
Trough	3rd quarter 1975	

Predicted:		
NIESR	Feb 1974	⎫ About a quarter way
Treasury	March 1974	⎬ through the downswing

1979–81		
Downswing	2nd quarter 1979	
Trough	3rd quarter 1981	

1979–81	*Date*	*Timing*
Predicted:		
NIESR	Aug 1979	
LBS	June 1979	⎫ About the start of
Treasury	June 1979	⎭ the downswing

1990–2		
Downswing	2nd quarter 1990	
Trough	1st quarter 1992	
Predicted:		
NIESR	Nov 1990	⎫ Six to nine months after
LBS	Feb 1991	⎭ the start of the downswing
Treasury	Nov 1989	Six months before the start of the downswing

8.1.3   Summary – Timing of Earliest Warnings

Inflations

1973–5	At the start of the rapid rise
1979–80	Six months after the start of the rapid rise
1989–90	Three months after the start of the rapid rise

Recessions

1970–1	Half way through the downswing
1974–5	About a quarter of the way through the downswing
1979–81	About the start of the downswing
1990–2	Six months before the start of the downswing

Only the warning of recession in 1990–2 preceded the start of the event and even that was unclear; in November 1989 the Treasury predicted that the growth of GDP between 1989 and 1990 would slow to 1.3 per cent, but a fall in GDP was not predicted until March 1991. Of the warnings of the other events, two coincided with the start of the event and the remaining four were sounded after the event had started.

8.2   PREDICTIONS MADE A FIXED PERIOD AHEAD

Another way of assessing the usefulness of forecasts is to compare outturns with forecasts that are made the same distance ahead of the year being forecast. This focuses attention on how a forecast for a fixed period ahead has changed rather than on the level of the new forecast. A change in direction, or an acceleration or deceleration, may contain valuable information. There have been examples of a forecast being useful in spite of its level being badly out.

A detailed analysis of the forecasts a fixed period ahead is contained in Appendix 8.2. The cyclical pattern of each type of forecast is compared to that of the outturn to see if there is a resemblance. If there is not the forecast is clearly useless. Assuming there is, the turning points of the forecast and the outturn are examined to establish leads and lags. A forecast with turning points that lag those of the outturn is only a genuine forecast if it is made twelve months or more prior to the start of the year being forecast; otherwise it is a reaction to something that has already begun to happen. A forecast with coincidental turning points is only a genuine forecast if it is made before the start of the year being forecast; otherwise it too is a reaction to something that has already begun to happen.

Table 8.1 gives a list of the forecasts of growth of GDP that bear a resemblance to outturns. It also indicates whether the turning points of the forecast have been leading, coincidental, indistinct or lagging. The final column gives an assessment of whether the forecast has been a genuine one or a report of something that has already started to happen. Table 8.2 does the same for forecasts of inflation.

8.2.1 Summary of Forecasts Made a Fixed Period Ahead

(i) Forecasts Made After the Start of the Year Being Forecast

Growth of GDP: resemblance was in general good but some of the turning points were indistinct and one lagged. The 'forecasts' are best described to be not wholly reliable reports of events that had already started to happen.
Inflation: in all cases resemblance was good and the turning points coincided. The 'forecasts' are best described as reliable reports of events that had already started to happen.

(ii) Forecasts Made Between Three Months in Advance and the Start of the Year Being Forecast

Growth of GDP: the Treasury's 'forecasts' were genuine forecasts but the turning points were not always distinct. LBS's forecast was satisfactory on only one out of three occasions. NIESR's were not of much value.
Inflation: Resemblance tended to be reasonable and the turning points tended to be coincidental but some lagged. The 'forecasts' are best described as rather unreliable genuine forecasts.

Table 8.1   Forecasts of growth of GDP bearing a resemblance to outturns – summary

	Resemblance between cyclical patterns	Leads/lags at turning points	Forecast/report
After the start of the year			
HMT 3 months after	good but indistinct between 1983 and 1988	5 coincidental, 1 indistinct	report
LBS 2 months after	good	2 coincidental, 1 indistinct	report
NIESR 2 months after	good	5 coincidental, 1 lagging	report
Just before the start of the year			
HMT 1 month prior	good but indistinct between 1983 and 1988	1 leading, 2 coincidental 1 indistinct	forecast
LBS 2 months prior	good until 1987, poor after	1 coincidental, 2 lagging	forecast before 1987
Earlier forecasts			
LBS 6 months prior	good until 1988, poor after	1 coincidental, 1 indistinct 1 lagging	forecast before 1988

Table 8.2   Forecasts of inflation bearing a resemblance to outturns – summary

	Resemblance between cyclical patterns	Leads/lags at at turning points	Forecast or report
After the start of the year			
HMT 3 months after	good	coincidental	report
LBS 2 months after	good	coincidental	report
NIESR 2 months after	good	coincidental	report
Just before the start of the year			
HMT 1 month prior	reasonable but amount of initial rises poor	2 coincidental, 2 lagging	unreliable forecast
LBS 2 months prior	quite good but too small a rise in 1990	2 coincidental, 1 lagging	forecast before 1991
NIESR 1 month prior	good prior to 1988, rise in 1990 missed	5 coincidental, 1 indistinct	forecast before 1988
Earlier forecasts			
LBS 6 months prior	quite good but lagging	2 indistinct, 1 lagging	report
NIESR 4 months prior	quite good	3 coincidental, 3 lagging	unreliable forecast
NIESR 7 months prior	quite good	1 coincidental, 1 indistinct 4 lagging	report

(iii)   Forecasts Made Between Six and Three Months in Advance of the Year Being Forecast

Growth of GDP: only one forecast was of value and that was LBS's warning of the 1980 recession.
Inflation: Resemblance was in general reasonable but some of the turning points lagged or were indistinct. The 'forecasts' are best described to be unreliable genuine forecasts.

(iv)   Forecasts Made More than Six Months in Advance of the Year Being Forecast

The cyclical patterns of the forecasts bore no resemblance to those of the outturns; forecasts this far in advance were useless.

8.3   CONCLUSIONS

The overall conclusion is that warnings of recession and inflation derived from the large macroeconomic models were sounded only a month or so before the start of the event. The Treasury had the best short-term forecasting record but even so its prediction of GDP lagged in 1989. LBS had a good record prior to 1986 but then slipped. NIESR's record can only be described as poor.

The record of forecasting inflation is particularly dismal. Inflation during the next few months should be relatively easy to predict because price rises in the pipeline can be directly monitored. Worldwide commodity prices and UK import prices can be scrutinised to predict wholesale input prices. Input prices and unit labour costs can then be used to predict wholesale output prices. Finally wholesale output prices can be used to predict retail prices. This pipeline-method can be used to forecast the behaviour of the retail price index during the next eight months or so. The macroeconomic models did not manage to achieve even this. Nevertheless this is the standard against which monetarist forecasts can be assessed.

APPENDIX 8.1   SEQUENCES OF FORECASTS – DETAIL

Both this appendix and Appendix 8.2 use graphical analysis. A formal statistical analysis is contained in Mills and Pepper (1997).

A.8.1.1   Forecasts of Inflation – Data

This appendix starts with an examination of the profiles of the three serious bouts of inflation since 1969. The data given below show the percentage rise in the retail price index (RPI) compared with the same quarter of the previous year.

1973–5 inflation (percentages)

1972 Q2	6.2	(low)
1972 Q4	7.7	
1973 Q3	9.2	(start of rapid rise)
1973 Q4	10.2	
1975 Q3	26.5	(peak)
1975 Q4	25.3	

1979–80 inflation (percentages)

1978 Q2	7.7	(low)
1978 Q4	8.1	(start of rapid rise)
1979 Q4	17.2	
1980 Q2	21.5	(peak)
1980 Q4	15.2	

1989–90 inflation (percentages)

1988 Q1	3.4	(low, ignoring 2.6 per cent for the third quarter of 1986)
1988 Q4	6.5	
1989 Q4	7.6	
1990 Q3	10.4	(peak)
1990 Q4	10.0	

A.8.1.2   Forecasts of Inflation – Predictions

(i)   The National Institute of Economic and Social Research
NIESR's four forecasts a year are published in the February, May, August and November editions of its *Quarterly Review*. For reference a complete record of the forecasts of inflation, starting with the ones made in 1970, is given in Table 8.17 in Appendix 8.3.

A general warning about consistency of data must be given. Some of
the predictions of inflation in the reference tables are for consumer prices;
others are for retail prices. Some are for calendar years, whereas others are
fourth quarterly comparisons or even half yearly ones. In the tables in
Appendix 8.3 there should be consistency up and down columns but there
may not be across rows. Details are given in the notes to the tables.

The charts that follow show how NIESR's predictions of inflation
progressed as a period of rising inflation approached. (The form of analysis is similar to that used in Barker 1985.)

Chart 8.1 introduces the presentation. It shows the sequences of
NIESR's predictions of inflation for 1974. The dates on which the predictions were made are along the bottom of the chart.

The first prediction was made in May 1973. This was wholly a forecast,
because the year being forecast had not yet started. The predictions in
August and November 1973 were also wholly forecasts for the same
reason. These wholly forecasts are shown by hollow triangles on the
graph. There were three of them.

The next prediction was made in February 1974. The year being forecast had started by then and some information about inflation during the
year had become available. The prediction was therefore based partly on
data for the year; that is, it was part forecast and part data. As the year
progressed more data became available and the predictions became less

Chart 8.1   NIESR – inflation: forecasts and data (for 1974)

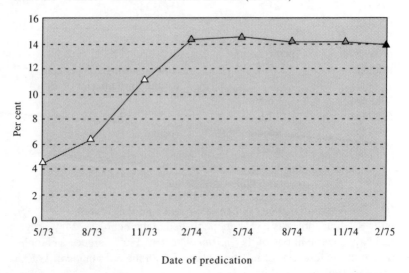

Date of predication

△ Forecasts   ⬕ Forecast/date   ▲ Data

forecasts and more data. Predictions that are part forecast and part data are shown by shaded triangles on the graph. There were four of them, the last being made in November 1974.

The final prediction shown in the chart is for February 1975. Full data for 1974 were by then available and the prediction has been deemed wholly data.[2] This is shown by a solid triangle on the graph. (The distinction between wholly forecast, part forecast and part data, and wholly data is used in Burrell and Hall 1993.)

Inflation in 1973, 1974 and 1975
Chart 8.2 shows NIESR's predictions of inflation for 1973, 1974 and 1975. The graph with squares shows those for 1973; the one with triangles and the slightly thicker line shows the predictions for 1974; and the one with circles shows those for 1975. The dates of the predictions are given along the bottom of the chart.

NIESR's first warning of a rise in inflation came in August 1973 when the prediction for 1973 was raised from the 5.0 per cent made in May to 9.5 per cent and that for 1974 was raised from 4.5 per cent to 6.4 per cent. In November the prediction for 1974 was raised to 10.6 per cent and in the following February to 14.5 per cent. (The data in this paragraph are an extreme example of the inconsistency mentioned earlier. The predictions made in May and August 1973 compared the fourth quarter of a year with the fourth quarter of the previous year. The one made in November 1973

Chart 8.2   NIESR – inflation: predictions for 1973, 1974 and 1975

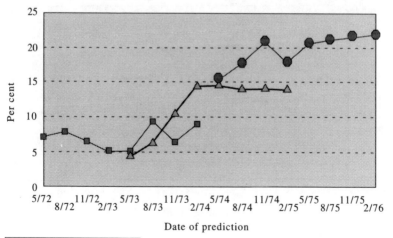

compared calendar years. That made in February 1974 compared second half of years. All the prices were however consumer prices.)

Inflation in 1979 and 1980
Chart 8.3 shows the sequences of NIESR's predictions of inflation for 1979 and 1980. The graph with the squares is for 1979; the one with the triangles and the slightly thicker line is for 1980.

The warning of the rise in inflation that was to occur in 1979–80 was made in August 1979 when the prediction for 1979 was raised from 10.5 per cent to 12.7 per cent and the one for 1980 was raised from 10.7 per cent to 13.8 per cent.

In the event inflation reached a peak in the second quarter of 1980, which explains why the graph with triangles subsequently falls.

Inflation in 1989 and 1990
Chart 8.4 shows the sequences of NIESR's predictions of inflation for 1989 and 1990. The graph with the squares is for 1989; the one with the triangles and the slightly thicker line is for 1990.

The warning of the inflation that was to occur in 1989–90 was made in May 1989 when the prediction for 1989 was raised from 5.8 per cent to 6.6 per cent. The warning of a further rise in 1990 came in February 1990 when the prediction for 1990 was raised to 6.8 per cent.

Chart 8.3   NIESR – inflation: predictions for 1979 and 1980

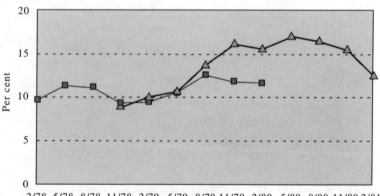

Date of prediction

1979   1980

Chart 8.4   NIESR – inflation: predictions for 1989 and 1990

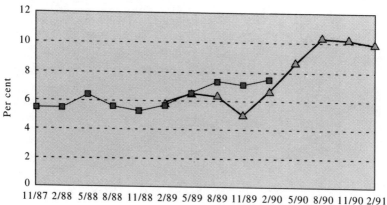

Date of prediction

■ 1989   ▲ 1990

(ii)   The London Business School

The Centre for Economic Forecasting at the London Business School publishes its three forecasts a year in its *Economic Outlook*, which is normally released in February, June and October. The first edition of *Economic Outlook* was published in January 1977.[3] A complete record of LBS's forecasts of inflation since then is given in Table 8.18 in Appendix 8.3.

Chart 8.5 shows the sequence of LBS's predictions of inflation for 1980. The display is the same as that in Chart 8.1 for NIESR, that is, hollow triangles are forecasts, shaded triangles are part forecasts and part data and the solid triangle is data. It will be seen that LBS predicts events further ahead than NIESR; there are no less than nine hollow triangles.

Inflation in 1979 and 1980

Chart 8.6 shows the sequences of the LBS's predictions of inflation for 1979 and 1980. The graph with the squares is for 1979; the one with the triangles and the slightly thicker line is for 1980; the display is again similar to that for NIESR.

Although LBS warned in April and October 1977 that inflation would rise in 1979 the warnings were subsequently reversed. The real warning came in June 1979, when the prediction for inflation in 1979 was raised from 9.8 per cent to 12.6 per cent and that for 1980 was increased from 10.4 per cent to 14.1 per cent. The prediction for 1980 was raised further in October 1979.

Chart 8.5 LBS – inflation: forecasts and data (1980)

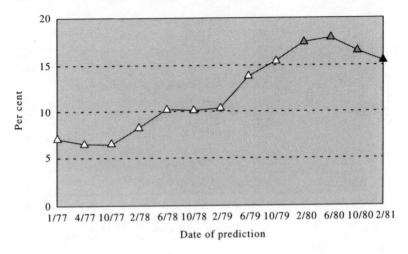

△ Forecasts ⬚ Forecast/data ▲ Data

Chart 8.6 LBS – inflation: predictions for 1979 and 1980

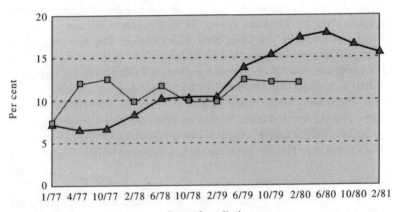

⬚ 1979 ⬚ 1980

Inflation in 1989 and 1990

Chart 8.7 shows the sequences of the LBS's predictions of inflation for 1989 and 1990. The graph with the squares is for 1989; the one with the triangles and the slightly thicker line is for 1990.

Chart 8.7   LBS – inflation: predictions for 1989 and 1990

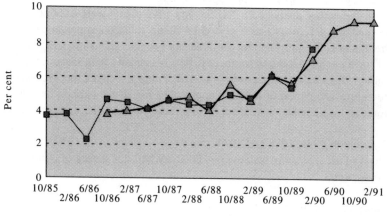

Date of prediction

1989   1990

Being charitable, we may note that the LBS warned that there was likely to be a slight rise in inflation in October 1988 when the prediction for 1989 was raised to 5.0 per cent and that for 1990 was increased to 5.6 per cent, but the warning of a substantial increase did not come until June 1989 when the predictions were increased to 6.1 per cent and 6.2 per cent respectively. Even so these predictions were considerably lower than the eventual outturns of 7.8 per cent and 9.5 per cent.

(iii)   The Treasury
HM Treasury started to publish its forecasts of inflation in December 1976. Since then two forecasts a year have been released. One of them is contained in the *Financial Statement and Budget Report* (FSBR) which was usually published in either March or April before the budget was changed from the spring to the autumn in 1993. The second of the two forecasts was released in the autumn, usually in November. It was first published in the Treasury's *Economic Progress Report* but this was subsequently altered to the *Autumn Statement* (AS) when the latter was introduced in 1982. After the budget was moved in 1993 the FSBR was published in the autumn and the second of the two forecasts was moved to the *Summer Economic Forecast* which was published in June. For reference, a complete record of the Treasury's forecasts of inflation for

The Validity of Monetarism

the fourth quarter of a year compared to the fourth quarter of the previous year is given in Table 8.19 in Appendix 8.3.

In the earlier analysis for NIESR and LBS charts were used showing sequences of forecasts as a period of rising inflation approached. This treatment is inappropriate for the Treasury because an insufficient number of forecasts are published for there to be a reasonably long sequence. Data rather than charts are accordingly used. Table 8.3 gives the Treasury's forecasts as a period of inflation approaches for all the periods for which forecasts were made, that is, not merely those between fourth quarters.

Inflation in 1973, 1974 and 1975
No data are available, because the Treasury had not started to publish its predictions.

Inflation in 1979 and 1980
The Treasury's warning of the rise in inflation that was to occur in 1979 and 1980 came in the FSBR in June 1979. The prediction in the *Autumn*

Table 8.3   Treasury forecasts of inflation
as a period of rising inflation approaches (RPI, percentages)

Period being forecast	Date of prediction						
	11/78	6/79	11/79	3/80	11/80		Outturn
1979–80 inflation							
1978 Q3 to 1979 Q3		**16.0**					**16.0**
1978 Q4 to 1979 Q4	**8.5**		17.5				**17.3**
1979 Q3 to 1980 Q3		13.5					
1979 Q4 to 1980 Q4			**14.0**	16.4	15.5		**15.3**
	3/88	11/88	3/89	11/89	3/90	11/90	Outturn
1989–90 inflation							
1988 Q2 to 1989 Q2	4.0						
1988 Q4 to 1989 Q4		**5.0**	**5.5**	7.5			**7.6**
1989 Q2 to 1990 Q2			4.5				
1989 Q4 to 1990 Q4				**5.8**	7.3	10.3	**10.0**

Sources: **Boldface**: *Memoranda on Official Economic Forecasting*, House of Commons Paper, 532–1, session 1990/1.
Remainder: *Financial Statement and Budget Report* and *Autumn Statement*, HMT, various.

Statement in the previous November was that RPI would be 8.5 per cent higher in the fourth quarter of 1979 than a year earlier; this was much too low. The prediction in June 1979 was that the RPI would be 16.0 per cent higher in the third quarter of 1979 than a year earlier. This prediction was more data than forecast.

Inflation in 1989 and 1990
The Treasury more or less failed to warn of the rise in inflation that was to occur in 1989 and 1990. In March 1989 the prediction in the FSBR was that the RPI would rise by 5.5 per cent between the fourth quarter of 1989 and a year earlier, which should be compared to the outturn of 7.6 per cent, and that the rise between the second quarter of 1990 and a year earlier would be 4.5 per cent. In November 1989 the forecast of inflation was raised but it was still much too low at 5.8 per cent for the year to the fourth quarter of 1990. In March 1990 this was revised to 7.3 per cent which should be compared to the outturn of 10.0 per cent.

A.8.1.3   Forecasts of Recession – Data

This section starts with the profiles of the four recessions since 1969. The data show the behaviour real GDP, coincidental indicators and unfilled job vacancies, together with conclusions about turning points. Data for unemployment are also given for 1969–71 because this recession is not clear from the data for GDP.

1970–1 Recession

	Data	Timing	Notes
Real GDP:			
'Peak'	76,099	1969 Q4	Does not fall for two
'Trough'	76,657	1971 Q1	consecutive quarters
Coincidental indicators:			
Peak	103.77	1969 Q2	
Trough	90.27	1972 Q1	
Unfilled job vacancies:			
Peak	203.2	1969 Q2	
Trough	120.5	1971 Q4	
Unemployment:			
Trough	570	1971 Jan	Ignoring 555 in May 1969
Peak	841	1972 March	
Conclusion:			
Downswing	1969 Q2		
Trough	1971 Q4		

1974–5 Recession

	Data	Timing	Notes
Real GDP:			
Peak	87 015	1973 Q3	Ignoring 87,119 in 1973 Q1
Trough	84 462	1975 Q3	Ignoring 84,434 in 1974 Q1
Coincidental indicators:			
Peak	113.9	1973 Q3	
Trough	88.6	1975 Q3	
Unfilled job vacancies:			
Peak	360.7	1973 Q4	
Trough	114.0	1976 Q1	
Conclusion:			
Downswing	1973 Q3		
Trough	1975 Q3		

1979–81 Recession

	Data	Timing	Notes
Real GDP:			
Peak	95,850	1979 Q2	
Trough	91,220	1981 Q3	Ignoring 91, 156 in 1980 Q4
Coincidental indicators:			
Peak	113.2	1979 Q2	
Trough	90.5	1981 Q1	
Unfilled job vacancies:			
Peak	251.7	1979 Q2	
Trough	81.9	1981 Q2	
Conclusion:			
Downswing	1979 Q2		
Trough	1981 Q3		

1990–2 Recession

	Data	Timing	Notes
Real GDP:			
Peak	120,581	1990 Q2	
Trough	116,136	1992 Q1	
Coincidental indicators:			
Peak	105.13	1990 Q2	Ignoring 107.07 in 1988 Q4
Trough	93.37	1992 Q1	
Unfilled job vacancies:			
Peak	255.2	1988 Q2	
Trough	108.10	1991 Q3	

Conclusion:
Downswing   1990 Q2
Trough   1992 Q1

A.8.1.4 Forecasts of Recession – Predictions

(i)   The National Institute of Economic and Social Research
A complete record of NIESR's forecasts of the growth of GDP in real terms, starting in 1969, is given in Table 8.20 in Appendix 8.3.

The warning about consistency of the data in the tables in Appendix 8.3 needs repeating. GDP can be measured in three ways; estimates can be based on data for expenditure, output or income, and the result may, or may not, be expressed as an average. Details are given in the notes to the tables. As with inflation there should be consistency up and down the columns of the tables but there may not be across rows.

Chart 8.8 shows NIESR's predictions of the growth in GDP for 1974. The display is similar to that for inflation and the dates of the predictions are the same. There are however two differences. The first is because data for GDP are not available as quickly as those for inflation and there is little information available in February about what has been happening to GDP since the start of the calendar year. The plot for February 1974 is

Chart 8.8   NIESR – growth of GDP: forecasts and data (for 1974)

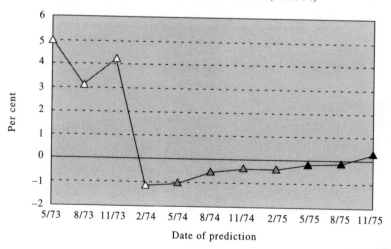

△ Forecasts ⊿ Forecast/data ▲ Data

accordingly shown as a hollow triangle for a forecast, rather than a shaded triangle for part forecast and part data. Similarly the plot for February 1975 is shown as a shaded triangle rather than a solid triangle. The second difference is because data for GDP are frequently revised. The revised data for 1974 are given in NIESR's *Quarterly Review* until the November 1975 edition; the solid triangles on the graph, indicating data, continue until then.

1970–1 Recession
Chart 8.9 shows NIESR's predictions of growth of GDP for 1970 and 1971. The squares are for 1970 and the triangles and the slightly thicker line are for 1971.

The warning of a slowdown came in August 1970 when the prediction of the growth of GDP in 1970 was reduced from 2.8 per cent to 1.7 per cent and the first prediction made for 1971 was 1.9 per cent. A warning of a more serious slowdown did not come until February 1971 when the prediction for 1971 was reduced to 1.1 per cent.

1974–5 Recession
Chart 8.10 shows NIESR's predictions of growth of GDP for 1974 and 1975, the squares being for 1974 with the triangles and the slightly thicker line for 1975.

Chart 8.9   NIESR – growth of GDP: predictions for 1970 and 1971

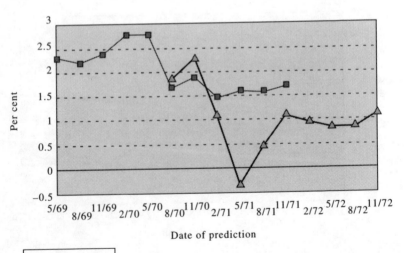

Chart 8.10   NIESR – growth of GDP: predictions for 1974 and 1975

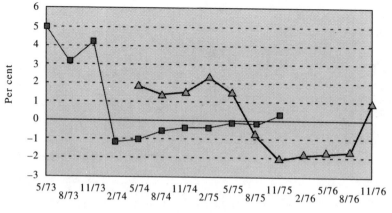

Date of prediction

1974   1975

The first warning of recession came in February 1974 when the prediction for 1974 was revised downward dramatically, from 4.2 per cent to −1.1 per cent. In May however a recovery was predicted for 1975. The warning of a deepening recession in 1975 did not come until August 1975, when the predicted growth of GDP was revised downward from 1.6 per cent to −0.7 per cent.

1979–81 Recession
Chart 8.11 shows NIESR's predictions of growth of GDP for 1979, 1980 and 1981. The squares are for 1979, the triangles for 1980 and the circles for 1981.

The first warning of a serious slowdown in growth came in August 1979 when the prediction for 1979 was revised down from 1.6 per cent to 0.5 per cent. The first warning of negative growth came in February 1980 when the prediction for 1980 was revised down from 0.2 per cent to −0.5 per cent. A forecast of negative growth in 1981 was not made until November 1980.

1990–2 Recession
Chart 8.12 shows NIESR's predictions of growth of GDP for 1990 and 1991. The squares are for 1990 and the triangles are for 1991.

The first clear warning of a slowdown came in November 1990 when the prediction of the growth of GDP in 1990 was revised from

Chart 8.11   NIESR – growth of GDP: predictions for 1979, 1980 and 1981

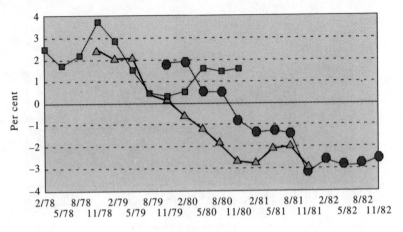

Date of prediction

1979 ■1979   △1980   ●1981

Chart 8.12   NIESR – growth of GDP: predictions for 1990 and 1991

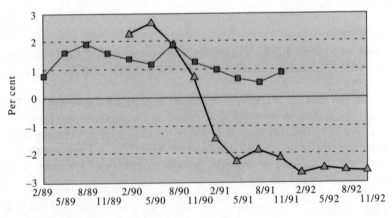

Date of prediction

■1990   △1991

1.9 per cent to 1.3 per cent and that for 1991 was revised from 1.9 per cent to 0.8 per cent. The warning of recession came in February 1991 when the prediction was revised downward from 0.8 per cent to −1.4 per cent.

(ii)   The London Business School

A complete record of LBS's forecasts of growth of GDP in real terms, starting in 1977, is given in Table 8.21 in Appendix 8.3.

Chart 8.13 shows LBS's predictions of the growth of GDP for 1980. The display is similar to Chart 8.8 for NIESR, except that there are more hollow triangles because LBS predicts events further ahead than NIESR There is also only one solid triangle for data, for June 1981. The solid triangles stop then because LBS's subsequent *Economic Reviews* did not include revised data for 1980. (The plot for February 1981 is shown as a shaded triangle for part forecast and part data because the data for GDP in 1980 were not yet available.)

1979–81 Recession

Chart 8.14 shows LBS's predictions of growth of GDP for 1979, 1980 and 1981. The squares are for 1979; the triangles are for 1980; and the circles are for 1981.

The warning of recession came in June 1979 when the prediction of the growth of GDP in 1980 was revised down from 3.0 per cent to

Chart 8.13   LBS – growth of GDP: forecasts and data (for 1980)

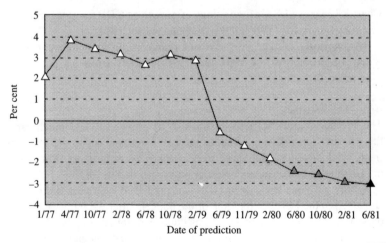

△ Forecasts   ◮ Forecast/data   ▲ Data

Chart 8.14   LBS – growth of GDP: predictions for 1979, 1980 and 1981

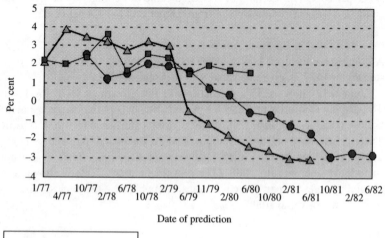

Date of prediction

■ 1979   ▲ 1980   ● 1981

–0.4 per cent. The first warning of negative growth in 1981 did not come until June 1980 when the prediction was revised down from 0.4 per cent to –0.4 per cent.

1990–2 Recession
Chart 8.15 shows LBS's predictions of growth of GDP for 1990 and 1991. The squares are for 1990 and the triangles are for 1991.

The warning of recession did not really come until February 1991 when the prediction for 1991 was revised down from 1.4 per cent to –0.8 per cent.

(iii)   The Treasury
The Treasury started to publish forecasts of growth of GDP much earlier than it did for inflation. The economic forecasts began in 1947 but from 1952 onwards qualitative indications only were given. Publication of quantitative forecasts on a regular basis resumed in 1968.

At first only one forecast of GDP was published each year and this was contained in the FSBR at the time of the budget. After the Industry Act was passed in 1975 a second forecast was published, initially in the Treasury's *Economic Progress Report*, then in the *Autumn Statement* and finally in the

Chart 8.15   LBS – Growth of GDP: predictions for 1990 and 1991

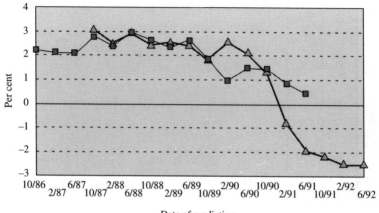

Date of prediction

▪ 1990   ▲ 1991

Summer Economic Forecast, as described for inflation. For reference, the complete record of the Treasury's forecasts of the growth of GDP in real terms for calendar years is given in Table 8.22 in Appendix 8.3.

Following the earlier treatment for inflation, data for the Treasury's forecasts of growth of GDP are given in tables rather than charts. Table 8.4 shows all of the Treasury's forecasts, that is, not merely those for calendar years, as a recession approaches.

1970–1 Recession
In April 1970 the Treasury was forecasting that the growth of GDP between 1969 and 1970 would be 3.5 per cent. They were also forecasting the same rate of growth between the first halves of 1970 and 1971. The forecast of a slowdown came in March 1971 when the latter prediction was revised downward to 1.3 per cent and 1 per cent growth was forecast between 1970 and 1971.

1974–5 Recession
The Treasury's forecast of recession came in March 1974 when a fall in GDP of 4.5 per cent was predicted between the first halves of 1973 and 1974, and a fall of 1 per cent was predicted between 1973 and 1974.

Table 8.4 Treasury forecasts of growth of GDP as a recession approaches (percentages)

Period forecast	FSBR	AS	FSBR	AS	FSBR	AS	FSBR	AS	FSBR	Outturn
					Date of prediction					
1970–71 recession	*4/69*		*4/70*		*3/71*		*3/72*		*3/73*	
1969 H1 to 1970 H1	2.9		3.1		1.6					
1969 H2 to 1970 H2			3.6		1.8					
1969 to 1970			**3.5**		1.7		1.7			**2.0**
1970 H1 to 1971 H1			3.5		1.3		0.3			
1970 H2 to 1971 H2					1.1		1.4			
1970 to 1971					**1.0**		0.8		1.1	**1.7**
1971 H1 to 1972 H1					3.1		3.9[a]		1.8[c]	
1974–75 recession	*3/73*		*3/74*		*4/75*		*4/76*			
1973 H1 to 1974 H1	4.5		-4.5[a]		-1.5[a]					
1973 H2 to 1974 H2			2.5[a]		1.5					
1973 to 1974			**-1.0**		-0.1		-0.2			**-1.5**
1974 H1 to 1975 H1					2.5[a]		0.5			
1974 H2 to 1975 H2					0.0		-3.5			
1974 to 1975					**1.5**		-1.7			**-0.8**
1975 H1 to 1976 H1					1.5		1.0			

Table 8.4   (Continued)

1979–81 recession	4/78	11/78	6/79	11/79	3/80	11/80	3/81	12/81	3/82	
1978 H1 to 1979 H1	3.0	2.9	1.0	0.2	0.9					
1978 H2 to 1979 H2		1.8	-0.5	1.0	1.5					
1978 to 1979		2.5	**0.5**							**2.8**
1979 H1 to 1980 H1			-1.0	-1.1	-2.0	1.3				
1979 H2 to 1980 H2				-2.6	-3.0	-1.3				
1979 to 1980				-2.0	**-2.5**	-4.6	-3.9	-2.0		**-2.0**
1980 H1 to 1981 H1					-1.5	-3.0	-2.4	-3.6		
1980 H2 to 1981 H2						-3.2	-3.8	-0.7	-0.5	
1980 to 1981						0.4	-0.2	-2.0	-2.0	**-1.2**

1990–92 recession	3/89	11/89	3/90	11/90	3/91	11/91	3/92	11/92	
1989 H1 to 1990 H1	2.5	1.0	1.4	2.0	-0.6				
1989 H2 to 1990 H2		1.6	0.6	0.0	0.5				
1989 to 1990		1.3	**1.0**						**0.5**
1990 H1 to 1991 H1			1.5	1.0	-3.1	0.8	-1.9		
1990 H2 to 1991 H2				-1.1	-0.7	-3.1	-2.5		
1990 to 1991				2.2	-2.0	-1.1	0.0	-2.5	**-2.0**
1991 H1 to 1992 H1				0.5	2.0	1.8		-1.0	

Note: [a] Affected by fuel shortages.

Sources: **Boldface**: *Memoranda on Official Economic Forecasting*, House of Commons Paper, 532–1, session 1990/1. Remainder: *Financial Statement and Budget Report and Autumn Statement*, HMT, various.

1979–81 Recession
The Treasury's forecast of recession came in June 1979 when a fall of
1.0 per cent in GDP was predicted between the first halves of 1979 and
1980.

1990–2 Recession
The Treasury started to forecast sluggishness in November 1989 when
1.3 per cent growth of GDP was predicted between 1989 and 1990. As
1990 progressed slow growth continued to be predicted. The first definite
forecast of a reduction in GDP came in March 1991 when a fall of 3.1 per
cent was predicted between the first halves of 1990 and 1991, and a fall
of 2 per cent was forecast between 1990 and 1991.

APPENDIX 8.2   PREDICTIONS MADE A FIXED PERIOD AHEAD –
DETAIL

This appendix compares outturns with forecasts made the same distance
ahead of the year being forecast. (When a forecast is published the focus is
on a column in the tables in Appendix 8.3, that is, on a vertical line. The
focus in Appendix 8.1 was on a row in the table, that is, on a horizontal
line. This appendix concentrates on diagonal lines.) This method of
judging forecasts focuses attention on how a forecast for a fixed period
ahead has changed rather than on the level of the new forecast. A change
in direction, or an acceleration or deceleration, may contain valuable
information.

The value of the method can be seen in Chart 8.16 (p. 84), which
shows the Treasury's predictions of the growth of GDP that were
made about three months after the start of the year being forecast,
together with the eventual outturns. (From 1994 onwards the forecast
has been contained in the *Summer Economic Forecast* published in
June; that is, it has been made six rather than three months after the
start of the year being forecast.) The graph with the shaded triangles
shows the predictions and the one with the solid circles and the slightly
thicker line shows the outturns. The code of shaded triangles for
predictions and solid circles for outturns is used in all of the charts in
this appendix.

If Chart 8.16 is examined it will be seen that the trough turning points
of the two graphs coincided in 1971. The prediction a year later was a
good one in terms of direction; the Treasury correctly reported that a
recovery was occurring. In terms of level the prediction was poor; growth
of 4.5 per cent was forecast compared to an outturn of 2.8 per cent. The

predictions in 1975 and 1979 were also good in terms of direction but poor in terms of level.

Chart 8.16 (overleaf) is the first of a series of graphs in this appendix that show forecasts made the same time ahead, or behind, the start of the year being forecast, together with the outturns. Each one of them is examined to see if:

(i) there is any resemblance between the cyclic patterns in the graphs for the forecasts and the outturns;

(ii) assuming there is, if the turning points of the forecasts lead or lag those of the outturns.

The resemblances and the leads and lags are then summarised in tables.

A.8.2.1 Treasury Predictions of Growth of GDP

In more detail and returning to Chart 8.16, it will be seen that the resemblance between the cyclical pattern of the forecast and that of the outturn was good except for between 1983 and 1988 when it was indistinct. The turning points tended to be coincidental.

Chart 8.17 shows the Treasury's forecasts of the growth of GDP made one month prior to the start of the year being forecast, that is, in November.[4] It will be seen that the resemblance between the cyclical patterns is much the same as that for the forecasts made three months after the start of the year being forecast and that the turning points also tend to be coincidental.

The resemblances between the Treasury's forecasts of the growth of GDP and the outturns are summarised in Table 8.5 (p. 85). Details of the leads and lags are given in Table 8.6.

Chart 8.16   HMT – growth of GDP: predictions three months after the start of
year and outturns

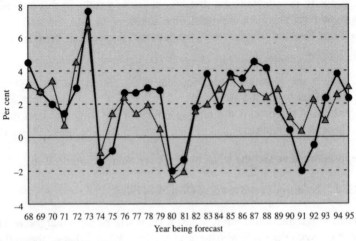

▲ Prediction (in March)   ● Outturn

Chart 8.17   HMT – growth of GDP: forecasts one month prior to start of year and
outturns

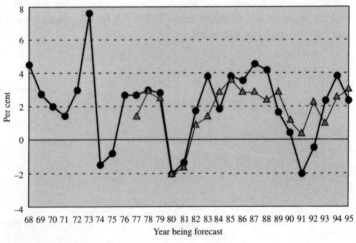

▲ Forecast (in Nov)   ● Outturn

Table 8.5   Treasury forecasts of growth of GDP – resemblances between cyclical patterns

Months in advance of year being forecast	Resemblance
3 months after	good but indistinct between 1983 and 1988
1 month	good but indistinct between 1983 and 1988

Table 8.6   Treasury forecasts of growth of GDP – leads and lags at turning points

Months in advance of year being forecast	1973 Peak	1974 Trough	1979 Peak	1980 Trough	1987 Peak	1991 Trough
3 months after	coincidental	coincidental	lead of 1 year[a]	coincidental	lead of 2 years[b] lag of 1 year[c]	coincidental
1 month	no forecast	no forecast	lead of 1 year	coincidental	lead of 2 years[b] lag of 2 years[c]	coincidental

Notes:
[a] The turning point of the forecast is clearer a year earlier than the outturn's.
[b] Indistinct turning point.
[c] When the turning point has become clear.

A.8.2.2   *Treasury Predictions of Inflation*

The Treasury's forecasts of inflation started to be published in December 1976. Chart 8.18 shows the ones made three months after the start of the year being forecast. Chart 8.19 shows those made one month prior to the start of the year being forecast. The resemblances between these forecasts of inflation and the outturns are summarised in Table 8.7 (p. 87). Details of the leads and lags at the turning points are given in Table 8.8.

Chart 8.18   HMT – inflation: predictions three months after the start of year and outturns

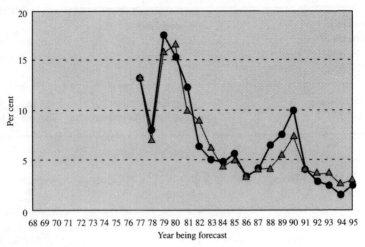

Chart 8.19   HMT – inflation: forecasts one month prior to start of year and outturns

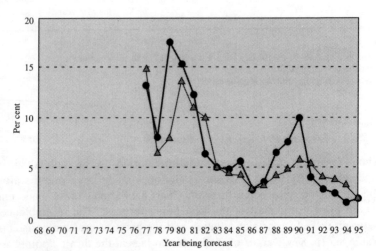

Table 8.7   Treasury forecasts of inflation – resemblances between cyclical patterns

Months in advance of year being forecast	Resemblance
3 months after	good
1 month	reasonable but amount of initial rises poor

Table 8.8   Treasury forecasts of inflation – leads and lags at turning points

Months in advance of year being forecast	1972 Trough	1975 Peak	1978 Trough	1979 Peak	1986 Trough	1990 Peak
3 months after	no forecast	no forecast	coincidental	coincidental[a]	coincidental	coincidental
1 month	no forecast	no forecast	coincidental	lag of 1 year	lag of 1 year	coincidental[b]

Notes:
[a] Being charitable.
[b] Indistinct turning point.

A.8.2.3   LBS Predictions of Growth of GDP

Chart 8.20 shows LBS's predictions of growth of GDP made two months after the start of the year being forecast, that is, in February. Chart 8.21 shows the forecasts made two months prior to the start of the year being forecast, that is in October. Charts 8.22 to 8.25 show LBS's predictions of growth of GDP made six, ten, 14 and 38 months prior to the start of the year.[5] Resemblances and details of leads and lags are given in Tables 8.9 and 8.10 (p. 91).

Chart 8.20   LBS – growth of GDP: predictions two months after the start of year
and outturns

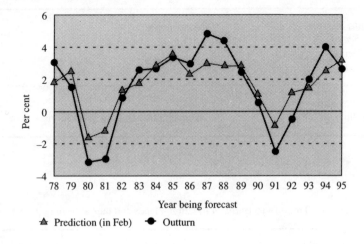

Year being forecast

▲ Prediction (in Feb)   ● Outturn

Chart 8.21   LBS – growth of GDP: forecasts two months prior to start of year
and outturns

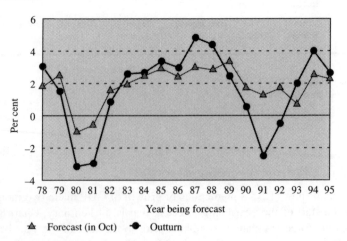

Year being forecast

▲ Forecast (in Oct)   ● Outturn

Chart 8.22   LBS – growth of GDP: forecasts six months prior to start of year and outturns

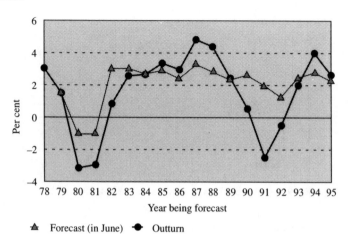

Chart 8.23   LBS – growth of GDP: forecasts ten months prior to start of year and outturns

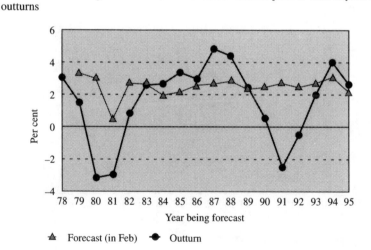

Chart 8.24   LBS – growth of GDP: forecasts 14 months prior to start of year and
outturns

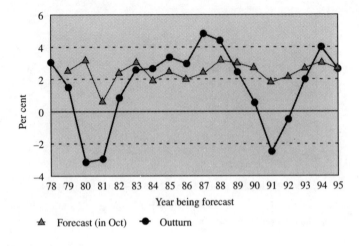

Chart 8.25   LBS – growth of GDP: forecasts 38 months prior to start of year and
outturns

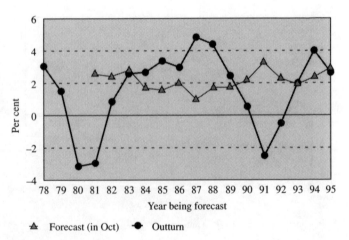

Table 8.9   LBS forecasts of growth of GDP – resemblances between cyclical patterns

Months in advance of year being forecast	Resemblance
2 months after	good
2 months	good until 1987, poor afterwards
6 months	good until 1987, poor afterwards
10 months	poor
14 months	poor
38 months	no resemblance

Table 8.10   LBS forecasts of growth of GDP leads and lags at turning points

Months in advance of year being forecast	1980 Trough	1987 Peak	1991 Trough
2 months after	coincidental	coincidental[a] lag of 2 years[b]	coincidental
2 months	coincidental	lag of 2 years	lag of 2 years
6 months	coincidental	indistinct	lag of 1 year
10 months	lag of 1 year	no relationship	no relationship
14 months	————cyclical relationship but very small amplitudes ————		
38 months	no forecast	no relationship	no relationship

Notes:
[a] Indistinct turning point.
[b] When the turning point has become clear.

A.8.2.4   LBS Predictions of Inflation

Chart 8.26 shows LBS's predictions of inflation made two months after the start of the year being forecast. Charts 8.27 to 8.33 show LBS's forecasts of inflation made 2, 6, 10, 14, 18, 22 and 38 months in advance. Resemblances and details of leads and lags are given in Tables 8.11 and 8.12 (pp. 96–7).

Chart 8.26   LBS – inflation: predictions two months after start of year and outturns

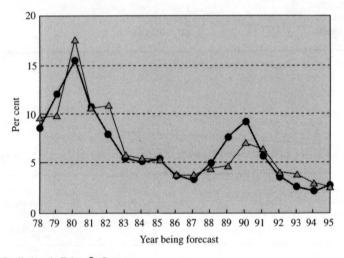

△ Prediction (in Feb) ● Outturn

Chart 8.27   LBS – inflation: forecasts two months prior to start of year and outturns

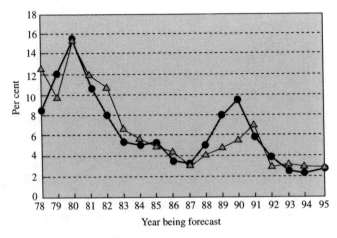

△ Prediction (in Oct)   ● Outturn

Chart 8.28   LBS – inflation: forecasts six months prior to start of year and outturns

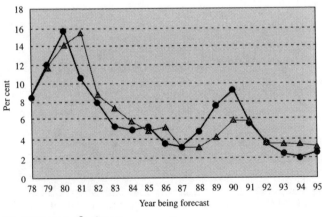

△ Forecast (in June)   ● Outturn

Chart 8.29   LBS – inflation: forecasts ten months prior to start of year and outturns

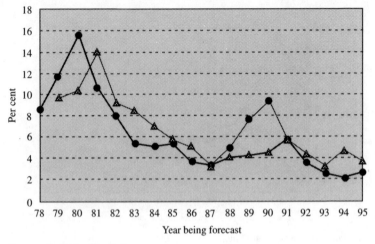

Chart 8.30   LBS – inflation: forecasts 14 months prior to start of year and outturns

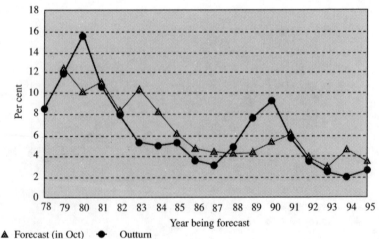

Chart 8.31   LBS – inflation: forecasts 18 months prior to start of year and outturns

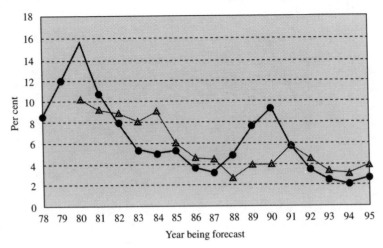

Forecast (in June)   Outturn

Chart 8.32   LBS – inflation: forecasts 22 months prior to start of year and outturns

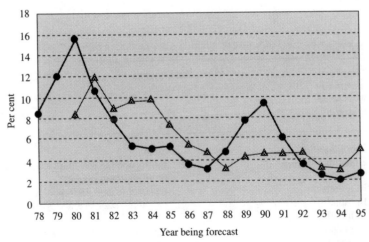

Forecast (in Feb)   Outturn

Chart 8.33   LBS – inflation: forecasts 38 months prior to start of year and outturns

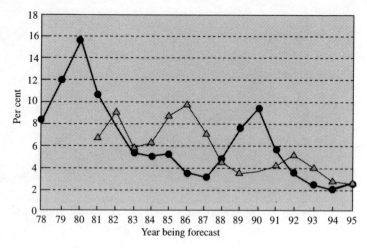

▲ Prediction (in Oct)   ● Outturn

Table 8.11   LBS forecasts of inflation – resemblances between cyclical patterns

Months in advance of year being forecast	*Resemblance*
2 months after	good
2 months	quite good but too small a rise in 1990
6 months	quite good but lagging
10 months	reasonable until 1988 poor afterwards
14 months	becoming poor overall
18 months	poor
22 months	poor
38 months	no resemblance

Table 8.12   LBS forecasts of inflation – leads and lags at turning points

Months in advance of year being forecast	1980 Peak	1987 Trough	1991 Peak
2 months after coincidental	coincidental	lead of 1 year[b]	coincidental[c]
2 months	coincidental	coincidental	lag of 1 year
6 months	lag of 1 year lag of 1 year[c]	coincidental[b]	coincidental[b] lag of 1 year[c]
10 months	lag of 1 year	coincidental	lag of 1 year
14 months	unclear[a]	lag of 1 year[b] lag of 2 years[c]	lag of 1 year
18 months	unclear[a]	lag of 1 year	lag of 1 year
22 months	unclear[a]	lag of 1 year	lag of 2 years
38 months	no forecast	no relationship	no relationship

Notes:
[a] Forecasts do not start soon enough.
[b] Indistinct turning point.
[c] When the turning point has become clear.

A.8.2.5   NIESR Predictions of Growth of GDP

Chart 8.34 show NIESR's prediction of growth of GDP made two months after the start of the year being forecast. Charts 8.35 to 8.39 show the forecasts made 1, 4, 7, 10 and 13 months prior to the start of the year.[6] Resemblances and details of leads and lags are given in Tables 8.13 and 8.14 (p. 101).

Chart 8.34   NIESR – growth of GDP: predictions two months after start of year and outturns

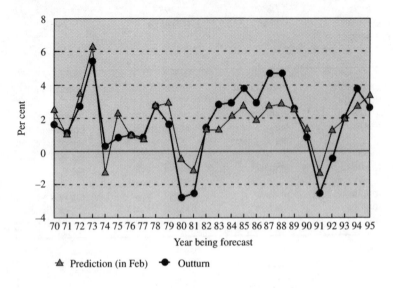

Chart 8.35   NIESR – growth of GDP: forecasts one month prior to start of year and outturns

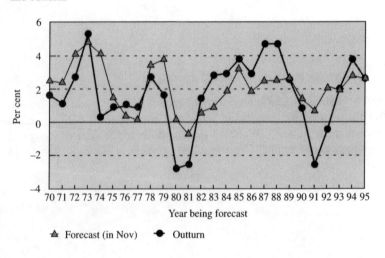

Chart 8.36   NIESR – growth of GDP: forecasts four months prior to start of year and outturns

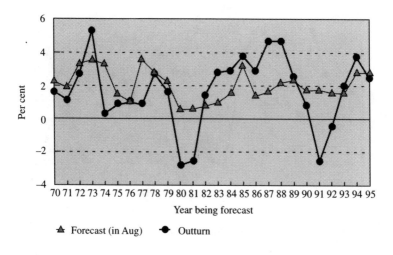

Chart 8.37   NIESR – growth of GDP: forecasts seven months prior to start of year and outturns

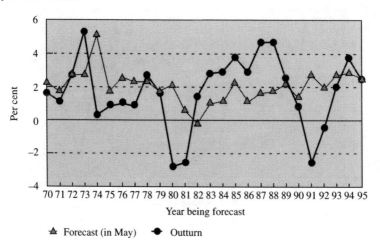

Chart 8.38   NIESR – growth of GDP: forecasts ten months prior to start of year
and outturns

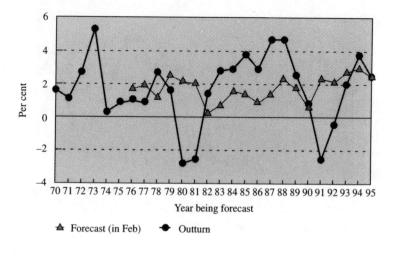

Chart 8.39   NIESR – growth of GDP: forecasts 13 months prior to start of year
and outturns

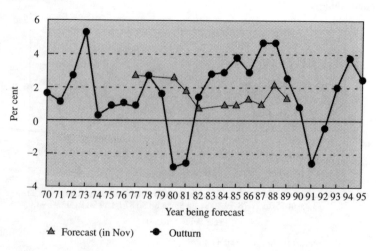

Table 8.13   NIESR forecasts of growth of GDP – resemblances between cyclical
patterns

Months in advance of year being forecast	Resemblance
2 months after	good
1 month	not very good
4 months	poor after 1981
7 months	poor
10 months	little resemblance
13 months	no resemblance

Table 8.14   NIESR forecasts of growth of GDP – leads and lags at turning points

Months in advance of year being forecast	1973 Peak	1974 Trough	1978 Peak	1980 Trough	1988 Peak	1991 Trough
2 months after	coincidental	coincidental	lag of 1 year	coincidental[a]	coincidental	coincidental
1 month	coincidental	lag of 3 years	lag of 1 year	coincidental[a]	lag of 1 year	coincidental
4 months	coincidental	lag of 2 years	lead of 1 year	coincidental	no relationship	no relationship
7 months	lag of 1 year	lag of 1 year	no relationship	no relationship	no relationship	no relationship
10 months	no forecast	no forecast	no relationship	no relationship	no relationship	no relationship
13 months	no forecast	no forecast	no forecast	no relationship	no relationship	no forecast

Note:
[a] Coincidental upswing.

A.8.2.6   NIESR Predictions of Inflation

Chart 8.40 show NIESR's predictions of inflation made two months after
the start of the year being forecast. Charts 8.41 to 8.45 show the forecasts
made one, four, seven, ten and 13 months in advance. Resemblance and
details of leads and lags are given in Tables 8.15 and 8.16 (pp. 105–6).

Chart 8.40   NIESR – inflation: predictions two months after start of year and
outturns

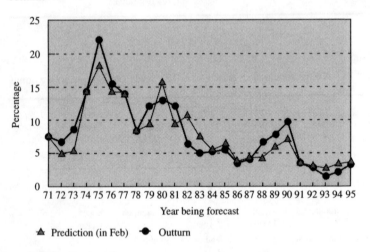

Chart 8.41   NIESR – inflation: forecasts one month prior to start of year and outturns

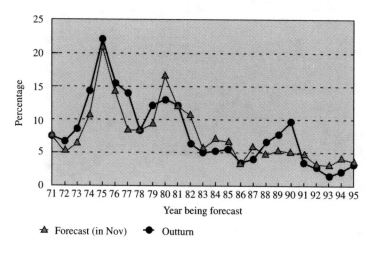

Chart 8.42   NIESR – inflation: forecasts four months prior to start of year and

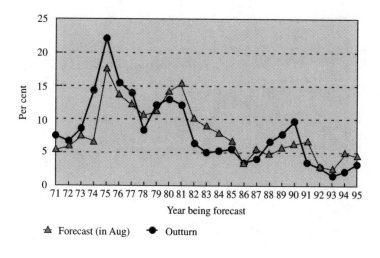

Chart 8.43   NIESR – inflation: forecasts seven months prior to start of year and outturns

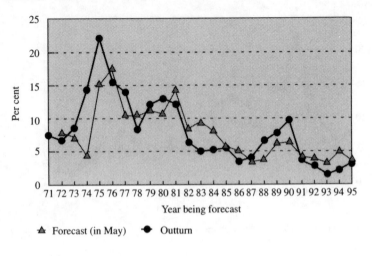

Chart 8.44   NIESR – inflation: forecasts ten months prior to start of year and outturns

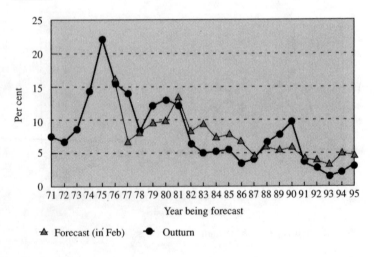

Chart 8.45   NIESR – inflation: forecasts 13 months prior to start of year and outturns

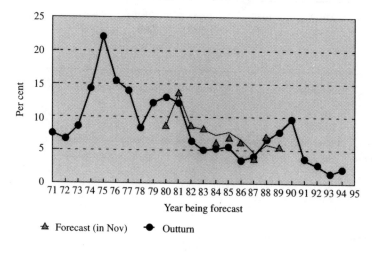

Table 8.15   NIESR forecasts of inflation – resemblances between cyclical patterns

Months in advance of year being forecast	Resemblance
2 months after	good
1 month	good prior to 1988, rise in 1990 missed
4 months	quite good
7 months	quite good
10 months	becoming poor
13 months	poor

The Validity of Monetarism

Table 8.16   NIESR forecasts of inflation – leads and lags at turning points

Months in advance of year being forecast	1972 Trough	1975 Peak	1978 Trough	1980 Peak	1986 Trough	1990 Peak
2 months after	coincidental[a] lag of 1 year[b]	coincidental	coincidental	coincidental	coincidental	coincidental
1 month	coincidental	coincidental	coincidental[a]	coincidental	coincidental	unclear
4 months	lag of 2 years	coincidental	coincidental	lag of 1 year	coincidental	lag of 1 year
7 months	lag of 2 years	lag of 1 year lag of 2 years[b]	coincidental[a]	lag of 1 year	lag of 1 year	coincidental
10 months	no forecast	no forecast	lead of 1 year	lag of 1 year	lag of 1 year	coincidental
13 months	no forecast	no forecast	no forecast	lag of 1 year	lag of 1 year	not clear

Notes:
[a] indistinct turning point.
[b] when the turning point has become clear.

APPENDIX 8.3   REFERENCE TABLES

The data given in the tables that follow may not be consistent. There should be consistency up and down columns but there may not be across rows. Attention is drawn to the notes.

Table 8.17   NIESR forecasts of inflation – reference table

Year of forecast	Date of forecast																		
	2/69	5/69	8/69	11/69	2/70	5/70	8/70	11/70	2/71	5/71	8/71	11/71	2/72	5/72[a]	8/72[a]	11/72[a]	2/73[a]	5/73[a]	8/73[a]
1968																			
1969					5.0	5.2	5.2												
1970					4.3	5.3	5.3	5.3											
1971							5.3	5.1	5.3	5.4	5.4	5.4							
1972								7.2	7.6	7.6	6.9	7.3	7.7	7.5	7.5	7.1			
1973									6.8	7.4	5.8	5.3	4.9	4.7	5.9	6.5	6.1	5.8	
1974														7.1	7.8	6.5	5.1	5.0	5.8
1975																		4.5	9.5
1976																			6.4
1977																			
1978																			
1979																			
1980																			
1981																			
1982																			
1983																			
1984																			
1985																			
1986																			
1987																			
1988																			
1989																			

Table 8.17 (Continued)

Year of forecast	11/73	2/74[b,c]	5/74	8/74	11/74	2/75	5/75	8/75	11/75	2/76	5/76	8/76	11/76	2/77	5/77	8/77	11/77	2/78	5/78
1968																			
1969																			
1970																			
1971																			
1972	6.4																		
1973	8.3	9.0																	
1974	10.6	14.5	8.6	8.6	8.7														
1975			14.7	14.3	14.3	14.1	14.5	14.5											
1976			15.2	17.8	20.9	18.0	20.7	21.3	21.8	22.1	22.1	22.1							
1977						16.0	17.5	14.1	14.4	14.6	16.6	15.9	13.2	15.6	15.2	15.2	15.4		
1978									8.4	7.1	10.6	12.7	8.5	14.2	14.5	15.0	13.9	14.5	14.3
1979														8.3	10.5	10.6	8.4	8.5	9.4
1980																		9.8	11.4
1981																			
1982																			
1983																			
1984																			
1985																			
1986																			
1987																			
1988																			
1989																			
1990																			
1991																			
1992																			
1993																			
1994																			
1995																			
1996																			
1997																			

Table 8.17 (Continued)

Year of forecast	Date of forecast																	
	8/78	11/78	2/79	5/79	8/79	11/79	2/80	5/80	8/80	11/80[c]	2/81[a]	5/81[a]	8/81[a]	11/81[d]	2/82[d]	5/82[d]	8/82[d,f]	11/82[d]
1968																		
1969																		
1970																		
1971																		
1972																		
1973																		
1974																		
1975																		
1976																		
1977	14.2																	
1978	9.3	8.0	8.2	8.6														
1979	11.2	9.5	9.6	10.5	8.5	8.4												
1980		9.2	10.2	10.7	12.7	12.0	11.9	12.0	12.1									
1981					13.8	16.3	15.8	17.2	16.7	15.8	12.9	12.8	12.8					
1982						13.4	13.0	14.9	15.3	11.7	9.6	10.5	10.5	12.0	11.9	11.9	11.9	11.9
1983										9.1	8.2	8.5	10.1	10.7	10.7	9.5	9.5	8.8
1984														8.3	9.5	8.7	8.7	5.8
1985																		6.0
1986																		
1987																		
1988																		
1989																		
1990																		
1991																		
1992																		
1993																		
1994																		
1995																		
1996																		
1997																		

Table 8.17 (Continued)

Year of forecast	2/83	5/83	8/83	11/83	2/84	5/84	8/84ᶜ	11/84ᶜ	2/85ᶜ	5/85ᶜ	8/85ᶜ	11/85ᵃ	2/86ᶜ	5/86ᶜ	8/86ᶜ	11/86ᶜ	2/87ᵃ	5/87ᵃ	8/87ᵃ
																	Date of forecast		
1968																			
1969																			
1970																			
1971																			
1972																			
1973																			
1974																			
1975																			
1976																			
1977																			
1978																			
1979																			
1980																			
1981																			
1982	8.6	6.2	6.2	6.2															
1983	7.6	6.5	5.5	5.2	5.4	5.4													
1984	7.2	8.0	7.5	6.8	5.6	5.3	5.0												
1985				6.8	7.5	6.0	5.7	5.0	4.8	4.8	4.8	5.1							
1986							6.5	6.5	6.5	5.3	5.5	4.8	5.5	5.5	5.5	5.5			
1987								6.0	6.5	5.0	3.5	3.4	4.0	2.8	3.3	3.8	3.5	3.4	3.4
1988												3.9	4.5	3.5	5.5	5.8	4.7	3.7	3.8
1989																6.8	5.9	4.1	4.9
1990																			
1991																			
1992																			
1993																			
1994																			
1995																			
1996																			
1997																			

Table 8.17 (*Continued*)

	Date of forecast																	
Year of forecast	*11/87ʳ*	*2/88ʳ*	*5/88ʳ*	*8/88ʳ*	*11/88ʳ*	*2/89ʳ*	*5/89ʳ*	*8/89ʳ*	*11/89ʳ*	*2/90ʳ*	*5/90ʳ*	*8/90ʳ*	*11/90ʳ*	*2/91ʳ*	*5/91ʳ*	*8/91ʳ*	*11/91ʳ*	*2/92ᵉ*
1968																		
1969																		
1970																		
1971																		
1972																		
1973																		
1974																		
1975																		
1976																		
1977																		
1978																		
1979																		
1980																		
1981																		
1982																		
1983																		
1984																		
1985																		
1986	4.1																	
1987	4.9	4.1	4.1	4.1	4.1													
1988	5.5	4.5	3.8	4.8	6.3	6.5	6.5	6.5	6.5									
1989		5.5	6.4	5.6	5.3	5.8	6.6	7.4	7.2	7.6	7.6	7.6	7.6					
1990						5.9	6.6	6.4	5.2	6.8	8.8	10.4	10.3	10.0	10.0	10.0	10.0	4.2
1991										4.6	4.7	6.9	4.9	4.2	4.1	4.1	3.9	3.4
1992														4.2	4.4	2.9	3.5	3.5
1993																		
1994																		
1995																		
1996																		
1997																		

Table 8.17 (Continued)

Year of forecast	Date of forecast															
	5/92[a]	8/92[c]	11/92[c]	2/93[a]	5/93[a]	8/93[c]	11/93[c]	2/94[c]	5/94[c]	8/94[c]	11/94[c]	2/95[c]	5/95[c]	8/95[c]	11/95[c]	2/96[c]
1968																
1984																
1985																
1986																
1987																
1988																
1989																
1990																
1991	4.1	4.1	4.1													
1992	3.6	3.6	3.4	2.7	3.1	3.1										
1993	3.3	2.8	3.4	3.0	2.8	2.3	3.0	1.5	1.5	1.5						
1994				5.1	5.1	4.9	2.0	3.7	3.3	3.2	1.6	2.6	2.6	2.6		
1995							4.3	4.6	3.9	4.5	2.2	3.9	4.0	3.2	2.6	3.2
1996											3.8	4.1	2.7	2.5	3.7	2.7
1997															3.0	3.5

Notes:

All figures are percentage changes in consumer price index, calendar year comparisons, except where shown.

a Percentage change in consumer price index, fourth quarter comparisons.

b Percentage change in consumer price index, second half year comparisons.

c Optimistic forecast.

d Percentage change in retail price index, calendar year comparisons.

e Percentage change in retail price index, fourth quarter comparisons.

f Assumed to be the same as the forecast made in 5/82.

In the charts the last figure for each year is taken as the outturn.

Source: National Institute Quarterly Review, NIESR.

Table 8.18 LBS forecasts of inflation – reference table

Year of forecast	1/77	4/77	10/77	2/78	6/78	10/78	2/79	6/79	10/79	2/80	6/80	10/80	2/81	6/81	10/81	2/82	6/82	10/82	2/83
1976	15.6																		
1977	12.4	14.9																	
1978	12.5	15.7	14.6	14.3	14.2														
1979	7.4	12.7	12.6	9.6	8.8	8.8	8.3	8.5											
1980	7.2	12.0	12.5	9.7	11.7	9.9	9.8	12.6	12.3	12.3	12.0								
1981		6.6	6.7	8.4	10.2	10.2	10.4	14.1	15.5	17.7	18.2	16.9	15.6	15.6	11.2				
1982			6.8	7.7	11.4	11.0	12.0	9.2	11.2	14.1	15.5	12.0	10.6	10.5	10.8	10.8	10.7		
1983						9.2	11.8	6.7	8.1	9.0	8.9	8.5	9.2	8.9	10.5	10.9	9.4	8.5	8.0
1984									6.0	7.7	7.5	6.5	9.7	8.1	10.9	8.5	7.4	6.8	5.8
1985												6.4	8.8	8.8	8.9	9.9	9.1	8.4	7.0
1986																9.6	11.2	9.3	7.5
1987																		9.9	7.8
1988																			
1989																			
1990																			
1991																			
1992																			
1993																			
1994																			

Date of forecast

Table 8.18 (Continued)

Year of forecast	*Date of forecast*																	
	6/83c	*10/83*	*2/84*	*6/84*	*10/86*	*2/85*	*6/85*	*10/85*	*2/86*	*6/86*	*10/86*	*2/87*	*6/87*	*10/87*	*2/88*	*6/88*	*10/88*	*2/89*
1976																		
1977																		
1978																		
1979																		
1980																		
1981																		
1982	8.0																	
1983	5.8	5.6																
1984	6.0	5.9	5.3	5.4														
1985	6.1	6.3	5.5	5.5	4.9	4.6	5.1											
1986	7.1	6.9	5.8	5.0	5.2	5.3	5.8	4.8	4.8	5.4								
1987		7.5	5.6	4.7	4.9	5.1	5.4	4.3	3.8	4.9	3.6	4.1	3.7					
1988			5.9	4.5	4.9	4.8	4.6	4.6	3.3	3.2	3.3	3.8	3.8	2.9	3.2	3.3		
1989					4.7	4.6	4.5	4.0	3.4	2.8	4.4	4.2	3.3	4.3	4.5	4.7	4.2	5.2
1990								3.7	3.8	2.2	4.6	4.5	4.1	4.6	4.4	4.4	5.0	4.8
1991											3.9	4.0	4.2	4.7	4.8	4.1	5.6	4.7
1992														4.4	4.7	4.0	5.9	4.8
1993																	5.5	5.3
1994																		

Table 8.18   (Continued)

Year of forecast	Date of forecast																	
	6/89	10/89	2/90[b]	6/90[b]	10/90[b]	2/91[b]	6/91[b]	10/91[b]	2/92[b]	6/92[b]	10/92[b]	2/93[c]	6/93[c]	10/93[c]	2/94[c]	6/94[c]	11/94[c]	2/95[c]
1976																		
1984																		
1985																		
1986																		
1987																		
1988	5.0																	
1989	6.1	5.5																
1990	6.2	5.8	7.8	7.8	9.5													
1991	6.0	6.5	7.2	9.0	7.1	9.5	9.5											
1992	5.5	5.5	5.9	6.1	4.2	6.6	5.5	5.7	5.9	5.9								
1993		4.5	4.9	4.7	3.2	4.6	3.8	3.2	4.2	4.2	3.8	3.7	3.7					
1994			4.9	4.2	3.1	3.5	3.5	3.3	3.4	3.8	3.3	4.0	3.5	3.2	2.7	2.7		
1995						3.3	3.7	3.4	3.3	3.3	4.9	4.9	3.7	3.1	3.1	2.5	2.1	2.4
1996								3.0	3.6	3.3	5.3	5.3	4.1	3.9	3.4	3.5	3.1	2.7
1997											3.7	3.7	4.8	4.1	3.3	3.6	3.4	3.0
1998														4.0	3.1	3.2	3.2	3.1
1999																	2.7	2.9

Table 8.18 (Continued)

Year of forecast	Date of forecast			
	5/95[c]	8/95[c]	11/95[c]	2/96[c]
1976				
1990				
1991				
1992				
1993				
1994	2.3			
1995	3.1	2.3	2.9	2.9
1996	3.1	3.2	3.0	3.0
1997	2.9	3.2	2.7	2.8
1998	2.7	3.0	2.5	2.7
1999		2.5	2.7	2.7

Notes:
[a] Percentage change in consumer price index, fourth quarter comparisons.
[b] Percentage change in retail price index, calendar year comparisons.
[c] Percentage change in retail price index, fourth quarter comparisons.

In the charts, the last figure for each year is taken as the outturn

Source: Economic Outlook, LBS.

Table 8.19   Treasury forecasts of inflation – reference table

Year of forecast	Date of Forecast																			
	12/76	3/77	10/77	4/78	11/78	6/79	11/79	3/80	11/80	3/81	12/81	3/82	11/82	3/83	11/83	3/84	11/84	3/85	11/85	3/86
1977	15.0	13.0	13.0																	
1978		13.5	7.0		8.0	8.1														
1979				6.5	8.5	16.0[a]	17.5	17.3												
1980							14.0	16.4	15.5	15.3										
1981								11.0	10.0	11.9										
1982										10.0	9.0									
1983												6.0	6.2							
1984												5.0	6.0	5.0	5.0					
1985														4.5	4.5	4.8	4.8			
1986																4.5	5.0		5.5	5.5
1987																			3.8	3.5
1988																				
1989																				
1990																				
1991																				
1992																				
1993																				
1994																				
1995																				

Table 8.19 (Continued)

Date of Forecast

Year of forecast	11/86	3/87	11/87	3/88	11/88	3/89	11/89	3/90	11/90	3/91	11/91	3/92	11/92	3/93	11/93	6/94	6/95	outcome
1977																		
1978																		
1979																		
1980																		
1981																		
1982																		
1983																		
1984																		
1985																		
1986	3.3	3.4																
1987	3.8	4.0	4.0	4.5														
1988			4.1	4.0	6.3	5.0												
1989					6.5	5.5	7.5	5.8										
1990							7.6	7.3	10.3	5.5								
1991									10.0	4.0	4.0							
1992											4.0	4.2	3.8					
1993												3.8	3.8	3.0				
1994													3.0	3.8	3.0	2.6	2.0	3.0
1995														3.3	2.8	2.5	1.5	2.4

Table 8.19 (Continued)

Notes:

Data show percentage change in the retail price index, fourth quarter comparisons.

From November 1992 mortgage interest payments excluded.

Final data in a row are outturns.

[a] Third quarter of 1979 compared with third quarter of 1978.

Sources:

Years being forecast	First autumn forecast	First 'spring' forecast	Second autumn forecast	Outturn
1977–81	MoEF	MoEF	EPR	MoEF
1982–90	MoEF	MoEF	AS	MoEF
1991–92	AS	FSBR	AS	ET
1993	AS	FSBR	FSBR	ET
1994–	FSBR	SEF	FSBR	ET

Codes: MoEF – *Memoranda on Economic Forecasting*, House of Commons Paper, 532–2, session 1990–1, pp. 32 and 35.

EPR – *Economic Progress Report*, HMT, various.

AS – Autumn Statement, HMT, various.

FSBR – *Financial Statement and Budget Report*, HMT, various.

ET – *Economic Trends*, CSO, June 1992 and June 1996.

SEF – *Summer Economic Forecast*, HMT, various.

Table 8.20 NIESR forecasts of growth of GDP – reference table

Year of forecast	Date of Forecast																		
	2/69	5/69	8/69	11/69	2/70	5/70	8/70	11/70	2/71	5/71	8/71	11/71	2/72	5/72	8/72	11/72	2/73	5/73	8/73
1968	3.7	3.8	3.3	3.4															
1969	3.3	2.2	2.2	2.0	2.0	1.9	1.9	1.9											
1970		2.3	2.2	2.4	2.8	2.8	1.7	1.9	1.5	1.6	1.6	1.7							
1971							1.9	2.3	1.1	-0.3	0.5	1.1	1.0	0.9	0.9	1.1			
1972									1.7	2.8	3.2	4.1	3.4	3.5	3.5	2.9	2.5	2.8	3.6
1973														2.8	3.5	4.9	6.3	6.9	6.6
1974																		5.0	3.1
1975																			
1976																			
1977																			
1978																			
1979																			
1980																			
1981																			
1982																			
1983																			
1984																			
1985																			
1986																			
1987																			

Table 8.20 (Continued)

| | | | | | | | | Date of Forecast | | | | | | | | | | |
Year of forecast	11/73	2/74	5/74	8/74	11/74	2/75	5/75	8/75	11/75	2/76	5/76	8/76	11/76	2/77	5/77	8/77	11/77	2/78	5/78
1968																			
1969																			
1970																			
1971																			
1972	2.7																		
1973	6.0	5.3	5.4	5.6	5.2														
1974	4.2	-1.1	-1.0	-0.5	-0.3	-0.3	-0.1	-0.1	0.3										
1975			1.9	1.4	1.6	2.4	1.6	-0.7	-2.0	-1.8	-1.7	-1.6	1.0						
1976						1.8	2.6	1.2	0.3	1.3	3.3	3.3	1.7						
1977									2.7	2.0	2.3	3.6	0.2	0.9	1.2	1.2			
1978														0.9	1.5	0.6	0.2	-0.1	0.8
1979														1.3	2.3	2.7	3.4	2.7	2.5
1980																		2.5	1.8
1981																			
1982																			
1983																			
1984																			
1985																			
1986																			
1987																			

Table 8.20 (Continued)

Year of forecast	Date of Forecast																	
	8/78	11/78	2/79	5/79	8/79	11/79	2/80	5/80	8/80	11/80	2/81	5/81	8/81	11/81	2/82	5/82	8/82[e]	11/82
1968																		
1969																		
1970																		
1971																		
1972																		
1973																		
1974																		
1975																		
1976																		
1977	1.0																	
1978	3.0	3.0																
1979	2.2	3.8	2.8															
1980		2.5	2.9	3.0	3.1	2.6												
1981			2.1	1.6	0.5	0.4	0.6											
1982				2.1	0.5	0.2	-0.5	1.7	1.6	1.7								
1983						1.9	2.0	-1.1	-1.8	-2.6	-2.7	-2.0	-1.9					
1984								0.6	0.6	-0.8	-1.3	-1.2	-1.3	-2.8	-2.5	-2.8	-2.8	-2.5
1985										0.8	0.2	-0.1	0.9	-3.1	1.4	1.0	1.0	-0.3
1986														0.6	0.7	1.1	1.1	1.0
1987																		1.0

Table 8.20 (Continued)

Year of forecast	Date of Forecast																		
	2/83	5/83	8/83	11/83	2/84	5/84	8/84	11/84	2/85	5/85	8/85	11/85	2/86	5/86	8/86	11/86	2/87	5/87	8/87
1968																			
1982	0.5	0.9	0.9	1.5															
1983	1.4	2.4	2.3	2.2	2.2	2.2	2.5	2.9											
1984	1.7	1.2	1.7	2.0	2.2	1.9	1.9	2.0	2.1	2.5	2.7	3.0							
1985				1.0	1.4	2.3	3.1	3.3	2.8	3.2	3.6	3.5	3.5	3.4	3.6	3.8			
1986								1.4	0.9	1.2	1.4	1.9	1.8	1.9	1.8	2.5	2.8	2.9	2.9
1987												1.1	1.4	1.7	1.8	2.4	2.8	2.9	3.3
1988																2.1	2.4	1.9	2.2
1989																			
1990																			
1991																			
1992																			
1993																			
1994																			
1995																			
1996																			
1997																			

124

Table 8.20 (Continued)

Year of forecast	11/87	2/88	5/88	8/88	11/88	2/89	5/89	8/89	11/89	2/90	5/90	8/90	11/90	2/91	5/91	8/91	11/91	2/92
1968																		
1981																		
1982																		
1983																		
1984																		
1985																		
1986	3.0																	
1987	4.0	4.7	4.8	4.8	4.7													
1988	2.4	2.9	3.5	3.9	5.4	4.7	4.3	4.4	4.7									
1989	1.5	1.9	2.2	2.4	2.6	2.5	2.3	2.4	2.3	2.5	2.6	2.5	2.5					
1990						0.8	1.6	1.9	1.6	1.4	1.2	1.9	1.3	1.0	0.7	0.6	0.9	
1991										2.3	2.7	1.9	0.8	-1.4	-2.2	-1.9	-2.1	-2.6
1992														2.1	2.0	1.7	2.1	1.3
1993																		2.7
1994																		
1995																		
1996																		
1997																		

Date of Forecast[a]

Table 8.20   (Continued)

								Date of Forecast								
Year of forecast	5/92	8/92	11/92	2/93	5/93	8/93	11/93	2/94	5/94	8/94	11/94	2/95	5/95	8/95	11/95	2/96
1968																
1991	-2.4	-2.5	-2.5													
1992	1.0	-0.5	-0.7	-0.7	-0.5	-0.5	-0.4									
1993	2.7	1.7	2.0	2.0	2.0	2.0	2.0	2.0	1.9	1.9	2.0					
1994				2.9	2.8	2.9	2.8	2.7	2.9	3.1	3.5	4.0	3.9	3.9	3.9	
1995								2.6	2.6	2.9	2.7	3.2	3.5	2.9	2.7	2.6
1996												2.5	2.6	2.5	2.4	2.4
1997																3.2

Notes:

All figures are the percentage growth of GDP at factor cost, calendar year comparisons, seasonally adjusted.

Forecast made at:
  2/69 to 5/73 – compromise estimate.
  8/73 to 2/81 and 11/81 to 2/93 – output based.
  5/81 to 8/81 and 5/93 to 2/96 – average measure.

In the chart the last figure for each year is taken to be the outturn for the year.

Source: National Institute Quarterly Review, NIESR.

Table 8.21   LBS forecasts of growth of GDP – reference table

Year of forecast	1/77ᵃ	4/77ᵃ	10/77	2/78ᵇ	6/78ᵇ	10/78ᵇ	2/79ᶜ	6/79	11/79	2/80	6/80	10/80	2/81	6/81	10/81	2/82	6/82	10/82	2/83ᶜ
1976	0.8	0.8																	
1977	1.8	0.7	0.8	0.7															
1978	2.0	1.7	1.7	1.9	1.5														
1979	2.2	2.0	2.4	3.5	2.4	3.0	3.0												
1980	2.1	3.9	3.5	3.2	1.8	2.6	2.4	3.0											
1981			2.5	1.2	2.8	3.2	3.0	1.6	2.0										
1982					1.6	2.1	2.0	-0.4	-1.1	1.8	1.7								
1983						2.4	2.3	1.7	0.8	-1.7	-2.3	-2.5	-2.9	-3.0					
1984								3.4	1.7	0.4	-0.4	-0.6	-1.2	-1.7	-2.9	-2.7	-2.8		
1985									2.7	2.4	1.9	2.4	2.6	2.8	1.7	1.5	1.0	0.3	0.5
1986										2.5	1.6	1.9	1.1	2.0	2.8	2.6	2.8	2.0	1.8
1987												1.8	1.4	1.4	1.8	1.8	2.2	2.0	2.0
1988															1.7	1.6	1.6	1.7	2.0
1989																		2.1	1.6
1990																			
1991																			
1992																			
1993																			
1994																			
1995																			

127

Table 8.21   (Continued)

	Date of Forecast																	
Year of forecast	6/83c	10/83c,d	2/84	6/84a	10/84c	2/85c	6/85c	10/85a	2/86c	6/86c	10/86c	2/87c	6/87c	10/87c	2/88c	6/88c	10/88c	2/89c
1976																		
1977																			
1978																			
1979																			
1980																			
1981																			
1982	0.9																	
1983	2.2	1.8	2.7	2.4														
1984	2.6	2.4	2.8	2.6	2.3	2.2												
1985	2.4	2.4	2.1	2.8	3.1	3.6	2.5											
1986	2.0	1.7	1.7	1.9	2.1	2.6	3.2	3.7	3.6	3.4								
1987		1.1	1.2	2.0	1.6	1.9	2.4	2.5	2.4	2.0	2.1	2.8	2.9					
1988					1.8	1.9	1.8	2.4	2.9	3.2	3.0	3.2	3.3	3.7	4.7	4.8		
1989							2.0	2.6	2.6	3.0	3.2	3.0	2.9	2.8	3.0	3.4	4.7	
1990								1.9	2.3	2.1	2.8	2.6	2.7	3.0	2.3	2.4	3.2	4.7
1991											2.2	2.1	2.1	2.8	2.4	3.0	2.7	3.0
1992														3.1	2.5	3.0	2.5	2.4
1993																	2.3	2.6
1994																		2.4

Table 8.21 (Continued)

Year of forecast						Date of Forecast[a]												
	6/89c	10/89c	2/90c	6/90c	10/90c	2/91	6/91	10/91	2/92	6/92	10/92	2/93	6/93	10/93	2/94	6/94	11/94	2/95
1976																		
1983																		
1984																		
1985																		
1986																		
1987																		
1988	4.3																	
1989	1.9	2.5	2.3															
1990	2.7	1.9	1.0	2.5														
1991	2.5	1.9	2.6	1.5	1.5	0.9	0.5											
1992	1.8	1.7	3.1	2.1	1.4	-0.8	-1.9	-2.1	-2.4	-2.4								
1993		2.0	2.2	2.3	2.2	2.4	1.6	1.9	1.2	0.1	-0.8	-0.8	-0.5					
1994				1.9	1.9	2.1	2.6	2.6	2.6	2.4	0.9	1.4	1.5	1.6	2.0	2.0		
1995					2.4	2.6	2.7	3.2	2.6	3.0	2.9	3.1	2.8	2.5	2.5	3.0	3.5	3.9
1996								2.9	2.8	3.0	1.7	2.7	2.7	2.6	2.2	2.3	2.5	3.0
1997											2.2	2.7	3.1	3.1	2.3	2.3	2.4	2.9
1998														2.7	2.4	2.7	2.8	2.8
1999																	2.6	3.0

Table 8.21 (Continued)

Year of forecast	Date of Forecast[a]			
	5/95	8/95	11/95	2/96
1976				
1990				
1991				
1992				
1993				
1994	3.8	3.9		
1995	2.9	2.8	2.7	2.6
1996	2.8	2.7	3.1	2.6
1997	3.0	2.7	2.8	2.8
1998	2.9	2.8	2.8	2.7
1999			2.6	2.5

Notes:

All figures are percentage changes in GDP, average measure, calendar year comparisons, except where marked.

[a] Expenditure based estimates.

[b] GDP at 1970 prices.

[c] Output based estimates.

[d] The 1987 forecast is assumed to be the same as that made in 2/84.

In the charts, the last figure for each year is taken as the outturn.

Source: Economic Outlook, LBS.

Table 8.22 Treasury forecasts of growth of GDP – reference table

Year of forecast	\<Date of Forecast\>																					
	3/68	11/68	4/69	11/69	4/70	11/70	3/71	11/71	3/72	11/72	3/73	11/73	3/74	11/74	4/75	11/75	4/76	12/76	3/77	10/77	4/78	11/78
1968	3.0																					
1969			2.5																			
1970				4.4			2.5															
1971						3.5	1.7		2.0													
1972							1.0		0.9		1.7											
1973									4.5		2.6											
1974											6.5	2.8										
1975												5.5		7.5								
1976												-1.0		-0.1		-1.5						
1977														1.5		1.4		1.3				
1978																2.5		2.0	-0.8	2.6		
1979																			1.2	0.3	0.7	2.6
1980																			1.5	3.0	2.0	3.0
1981																						2.5
1982																						
1983																						
1984																						
1985																						
1986																						
1987																						
1988																						
1989																						

Table 8.22 (Continued)

Year of forecast	Date of forecast																			
	6/79	11/79	3/80	11/80	3/81	12/81	3/82	11/82	3/83	11/83	3/84	11/84	3/85	11/85	3/86	11/86	3/87	11/87	3/88	11/88
1968																				
1969																				
1970																				
1971																				
1972																				
1973																				
1974																				
1975																				
1976																				
1977																				
1978	2.9	2.9																		
1979	0.5	1.0	1.5	2.8																
1980		-2.0	-2.5	-3.0	-2.5	-2.0														
1981				-1.5	-2.0	-2.0	-2.0	-1.2												
1982						1.0	1.5	0.5	0.5	1.7										
1983								1.5	2.0	3.0	3.0	3.8								
1984										3.0	3.0	2.5	2.5	1.8						
1985												3.5	3.5	3.5	3.5	3.8				
1986														3.0	3.0	2.5	2.5	3.6		
1987																3.0	3.0	4.0	4.5	4.4
1988																		2.5	3.0	4.5
1989																				3.0

Table 8.22   (Continued)

Year of forecast	3/89	11/89	3/90	11/90	3/91	11/91	3/92	11/92	3/93	11/93	6/94	11/94	6/95	outcome
						Date of forecast								
1968														
1980														
1981														
1982														
1983														
1984														
1985														
1986														
1987														
1988	4.5	4.2												
1989	2.5	2.0	2.3											
1990		1.3	1.0	1.7										
1991				1.0	0.5	0.5								
1992				0.5	-2.0	-2.0	-2.5	-2.0						
1993						2.3	1.0	-1.0	-0.5	-0.5	2.0	2.3		
1994								1.0	1.3	1.8	2.8	4.0	3.9	
1995										2.5	2.8	3.3	3.0	2.3

Table 8.22 (Continued)

Notes:
Final data in a row are outturns.
Data show percentage growth of GDP at factor cost, calendar year comparisons.

Sources:

Years being forecast	First autumn forecast	First 'spring' forecast	Second autumn forecast	Second 'spring' prediction	Outturn
1968–9	n.a.	MoEF	n.a.	n.a.	MoEF
1970–5	n.a.	MoEF	n.a.	FSBR	MoEF
1976	n.a.	MoEF	MoEF	FSBR	MoEF
1977–90	MoEF	MoEF	MoEF	FSBR	MoEF
1991–2	AS	FSBR	AS	FSBR	ET
1993	AS	FSBR	FSBR	FSBR	ET
1994–	FSBR	SEF	FSBR	SEF	ET

Codes: MoEF – *Memoranda on Economic Forecasting*, House of Commons Paper, 532-2, session 1990–1, pp. 32 and 35.
AS – *Autumn Statement*, HMT, various.
FSBR – *Financial Statement and Budget Report*, HMT, various.
ET – calculated from *Economic Trends*, CSO, June 1996, p. 6.
SEF – *Summer Economic Forest*, HMT, various.

9 A Monetarist Forecast

The library of Greenwell *Monetary Bulletins*, circulars, articles and speeches by the author consists of nearly 350 items. A survey of the predictions of which there is a written record is given in Appendix 9.1. The results are summarised below.

The four recessions and three inflations identified in Chapter 7 were all forecast to a greater or lesser extent, but not their precise timing. Some of the major crises in financial market that enforced policy changes were also forecast. There were however some predictions of events that did not occur and it is hard to make sure that all of these have been included in the survey. The author is no exception to the rule that nearly all forecasters remember their successes and conveniently forget their failures.

9.1 SUMMARY – FORECASTS THAT WERE BASICALLY CORRECT

In considering what follows it should be appreciated that the author was particularly concerned about two harmful economic occurrences. The first was a rise in unemployment. The second was high inflation. The two are connected. If inflation is allowed to accelerate a recession becomes a necessary remedial measure. Unemployment will then rise. If this rise is to be prevented the earlier acceleration of inflation must not be allowed to occur. The *Bulletin*, therefore, criticised the government whenever inflationary pressure had been allowed to build up. It was also critical when a recession was in danger of becoming unnecessarily deep or prolonged. If this approach is adopted warnings of inflation should be made at an early stage of a business cycle but those of an unnecessarily deep recession will be sounded at a fairly late stage.

Assessment of the dangers was based on the behaviour of the money supply adjusted for identified distortions. Warnings of inflation were made whenever excessive monetary growth had been allowed to occur for more than about six months. Warnings of an unnecessarily deep recession were made whenever inadequate monetary growth had persisted for longer than about six months. The detail of the method is described in Chapter 11.

9.1.1   The Record – Inflations

1973–5	*Date*	*First warning*
Start of rapid rise	1973 Q3	
Peak	1975 Q3	

Predicted:
NIESR		Aug 1973
Greenwell		**April 1972** (see Section A.9.1.2, p. 139)

1979–80		
Start of rapid rise	1978 Q4	
Peak	1980 Q2	

Predicted:
NIESR		Aug 1979
LBS		June 1979
Treasury		June 1979
Greenwell		**April 1978** (see Section A.9.1.6, p. 145)

1989–90		
Start of rapid rise	1988 Q4	
Peak	1990 Q3	

Predicted:
NIESR		May 1989
LBS		June 1989
Treasury		March 1990
Greenwell		**Aug 1987** (see Section A.9.1.9, p. 151)

9.1.2   The Record – Recessions

1970–1	*Date*	*Early warning*	*Warning about depth*
Downswing	1969 Q2		
Trough	1971 Q4		

Predicted:
NIESR		Aug 1970	
Treasury		March 1971	
Greenwell		**Oct 1969** (see Section A.9.1.1, p. 139)	

1974–5			
Downswing	1973 Q3		
Trough	1975 Q3		

Predicted:
NIESR		Feb 1974	
Treasury		March 1974	
Greenwell		**Dec 1973**	**April 1974**

(see Section A.9.1.3, p. 141)

1979–81	Date	Early warning	Warning about depth
Downswing	1979 Q2		
Trough	1981 Q3		

Predicted:
NIESR		Aug 1979	
LBS		June 1979	
Treasury		June 1979	
Greenwell		**Aug 1979**	**May 1980**

(see Section A.9.1.7 p. 147)

1990–2			
Downswing	1990 Q2		
Trough	1992 Q1		

Predicted:
NIESR		Nov 1990	
LBS		Feb 1991	
Treasury		Nov 1990	
Greenwell/Liverpool Six'		**Nov 1988**	**Feb 1991**

(see Section A.9.1.12, p. 54)

9.1.3   The Record – Financial Crises

1976 Sterling Crisis   Warning
October 1976

Predicted:
Greenwell   **April 1976** (see Section A.9.1.4, p. 142)

1987 Stock Market Crash
October 1987

Predicted:
Greenwell   **Sept 1987** (see Section A.9.1.10, p. 152)

9.2   SUMMARY – FORECASTS THAT WERE INCORRECT AND 'WOBBLES'

9.2.1   Incorrect Prediction in 1977 of Recession After the IMF Measures

After the IMF measures in October 1976 the monetary squeeze did not last as long as the author expected. Tighter fiscal policy was offset by money pouring back from abroad. The economy merely slowed (the coincidental indicators in fact fell from 100.4 in the fourth quarter of 1976 to 97.7 in the third quarter of 1977, as shown on Chart 7.1). The forecast of recession in the *Bulletin* was reversed in October 1977 (see Section A.9.1.5, p. 144).

9.2.2 Unfounded Worries in the Early 1980s About Inflation

In late 1981 and in 1982 the *Bulletins* expressed concern about inflation but more about problems that were being built up in the future than about the present (see Section A.9.1.8, p. 148).

9.2.3 'Wobble' After the Stock Market Crash in October 1987

There was a 'wobble' after the stock market crash in October 1987. The *Bulletins* expressed concern more about the US than the UK. A recession was forecast in the US and worries were expressed about the effect that this would have on the UK (see Section A.9.1.11, p. 152).

9.3 ASSESSMENT

The record shows that the author, in spite of trying to predict only major events, made too many forecasts. The explanation is his desire to compete with other forecasters. By their nature, predictions of major events will be made only occasionally. One having waited while others were making routine forecasts, there was a great temptation to try to be first with a forecast of a major event. This meant that predictions were made when it would have been wiser to wait until the situation had become clearer.

The lesson is that the temptation to be first should be resisted. The aim should be reliability. Forecasts should be made infrequently. The difficulty is that they will not be noticed because of lack of regular publicity, as explained in Section 6.4, p. 52.

Subject to this qualification the warnings of inflationary pressure were reasonably satisfactory. Some may argue that they were given too early, but such an accusation is almost inevitable if they are to be given in time for remedial action to be taken, remembering that the seeds of inflation are sown some two years before it materialises.

The warnings about recessions are more difficult to judge. The early warnings of the 1970–1 and 1974–5 recessions were satisfactory. The warning that the 1974–5 recession would deepen was made in April 1974. This should be compared with the forecast made by the Treasury at the end of March that GDP would grow by 1.5 per cent between 1974 and 1975 and the forecast made by NIESR in May that the growth would be 1.9 per cent. As the trough of the recession actually occurred in the third quarter of 1975 the *Bulletin's* warning that the recession would last longer than the Treasury and NIESR were predicting was correct.

The *Bulletin's* early warning of the 1979–81 recession was late. It was made in August 1979, at the same time as NIESR's, but this was two months after the warnings sounded by LBS and the Treasury. The *Bulletin's* warning that the recession would deepen was made in May 1980 and was a good one. In the same month NIESR predicted growth of 0.6 per cent between 1980 and 1981; their forecast of a fall did not come until November. LBS first forecast a fall in GDP in 1981 (0.6 per cent) in June 1980; their forecasts were subsequently revised steadily downward to –2.9 per cent in October 1981. (The Treasury's first forecast for 1981 was made in November 1980; it was that GDP would fall by 1.5 per cent.)

Turning to the 1990–2 recession, the first warning in a *Bulletin* that there was a danger that debt-deflation would lead to a recession was in November 1988. There is no doubt that this was crying wolf too soon (see Section A.9.1.12, p. 154 for the warning and Section 3.6, p. 25 for Nigel Lawson's observations about it) but other forecasters did not give any prior warning. The author, as one of the 'Liverpool Six' (described in Chapter 10), was party to the warning of deepening recession in the first letter to *The Times* from the 'Six' in February 1991 (see Section A.9.1.12, p. 154). In the same month NIESR forecast that the recession would be short-lived, more precisely that GDP would rise by 2.1 per cent between 1990 and 1991. LBS's predictions for the same year, also made in February, was a rise of 2.4 per cent. The Treasury's first forecast for 1991 was made in November 1990. It was that GDP would rise by 0.5 per cent but by March 1991 the forecast had been altered to a fall of 2.0 per cent. It should be remembered that at the time the UK was within the Exchange Rate Mechanism (ERM) of the European Monetary System and the Liverpool Six were alarmed by the height of interest rates that were needed to maintain sterling's exchange rate because this height had already lead to inadequate monetary growth. The extreme concern was about what would happen if the UK remained in ERM. In the event we were forced out, interest rates fell and the economy started to recover. This was an occasion when monetarists were clearly in the right.

9.4   CONCLUSION

The overall conclusion is that the approach to economic forecasting developed in the Greenwell *Monetary Bulletin* had a reasonably good track record of predicting major economic events but not the precise timing of an event. The record was better than that of the largely Keynesian macro-economic models.

Recapitulating on Chapter 4, because control of the money supply was not seriously attempted in the 1980s, monetarism cannot be judged by the outcome and the next strongest test is the forecasting record using monetary analysis. The conclusion of this chapter is that monetarism passed this second test. The popular impression that monetarism was tried in the 1980s, was found wanting and failed is wrong. This conclusion is strengthened as a result of developments described in the third part of this book.

APPENDIX 9.1 THE RECORD IN DETAIL

This appendix contains predictions from the survey of the library of Greenwell *Monetary Bulletins*, circulars, articles and speeches by the author. The month of circulation of the item from which the quotation is taken is given before the title of the item and, to assist anyone trying to audit the author's forecasting record, the number of the page containing the quotation is given in brackets immediately after the end of the quotation. The selection of quotations is by no means exhaustive.

A.9.1.1 *Prediction of the 1970–1 Recession*

October 1969 – Oral Contribution at a Sessional Meeting of the Institute of Actuaries (see Section 2.9, p. 11)

'If a person were a Friedman follower in the United Kingdom that person would forecast a very bad slump indeed about the spring and summer of next year. However, if that person turned to an independent measure of the velocity of circulation, he would see that the velocity of circulation in the United Kingdom had expanded at a truly dramatic rate during the last four or five months, and that more or less illustrated the City of London was too efficient for the money supply argument to work.' (*Journal of the Institute of Actuaries*, vol. 96, 1970, p. 45)

A.9.1.2 *Prediction of the 1973–5 Inflation*

April 1972 – 'Impressions after the Budget'

'The Chancellor has proposed the fourth fiscal package since the Conservative Party came into office under two years ago. In his latest exercise, he has totally ignored the lengthening time lags before his previous measures will work ... a public sector borrowing requirement of a massive

£3358 million during 1972/3, which implies a probable growth in the money supply of 20% in the coming twelve months and an extraordinary 50% in the three years to March 1973. He has, in effect, made sure that the economy will grow even at a faster pace than his target rate of 5 per cent.' (p. 1)

'In the budget speech the Chancellor forecast that the rate of growth of G.D.P. would have fallen from 5 per cent p.a. during the second half of 1971 to 3 per cent p.a. by the end of 1972 ...' (p. 3)

'The other important economic forecast is by the National Institute of Economic and Social Research which in its February forecast is even more pessimistic than the Chancellor ...' (p. 4)

'Conclusions:
1. The Treasury is too low in its forecast of 5 per cent p.a. growth of G.D.P. in real terms from the second half of 1971 to the first half of 1973. This is because the Treasury has underestimated the strength of the reflationary forces at work and overestimated the amount of fiscal drag.
2. Because of the sluggish response of the U.K. economy, the Treasury's forecast is likely to be correct initially, say during the next six months. After this initial period the growth of G.D.P. in money terms is likely to accelerate rapidly.' (p. 7)

January 1973 – Speech at a Meeting of the Society of Investment Analysts

'The economy is at present growing at about 5 per cent. In my opinion it will continue to do so during the next eighteen months or so. I base this forecast mainly on two factors. History shows that economies develop considerable momentum of their own – witness the long reaction time of the U.K. economy to official measures. Secondly, the growth of the money supply, which has a good track record of forecasting the U.K. economy over the last few years, is directly contrary to the view that the internal economic forces are decelerating.' (p. 5)

March 1973 – Budget Comment

'What is of immediate concern is the very serious consequences of financing the public sector deficit by excessive recourse to the banking system and, therefore, expansion of the money supply ...' (p. 1)

'Conclusions:
The immediate problem facing the Chancellor is to finance the public sector's borrowing requirement without relying heavily on the banking system. The budget has recognised the urgency and importance of the problem by introducing measures to increase savings by the non-bank sector which we find to be totally inadequate. The prospect of faster growth in the money supply at this stage of the economic cycle is indeed

disturbing. It is no less than the undermining of the Prices and Incomes Policy, continuing pressure on sterling to float lower, and the need for a sharp and dangerous reversal of monetary and fiscal policy when the economy eventually, but inevitably, reaches full employment.' (p. 5)

September 1973 – Monetary Bulletin, no. 16

'The Treasury, the Bank of England and the National Institute of Economic and Social Research all appear to consider that the economy is naturally decelerating. The lack of buoyancy in consumer demand is being cited as evidence that this forecast is correct. The monetary forecast is in disagreement. The monetary pressures on the economy do not appear to be decelerating significantly. The monetary forecast is that home demand will not reduce sufficiently to provide the necessary resources for export and manufacturing investment. There is a fear that the lull in consumer expenditure will prove to be only temporary.' (p. 3)

A.9.1.3   Predictions of the 1974–5 Recession

December 1973 – 'The Impact of an Oil Shortage on the General Economic Situation and Interest Rates' (with Harold Rose)

'As 1974 develops, however, the need to check demand will be replaced by the need to support it, and on an international scale. Easier monetary policies will, therefore, be required in the course of the next year; for otherwise there is a danger that the eventual decline in activity will be magnified as illiquidity brought about by a fall in profits due to shortages, or to reduced demand, spreads. Indeed, by the end of 1974 a reflationary budget might well be needed.' (p. 6)

January 1974 – Bulletin, no. 20

'Our note of the 4th December "The impact of an oil shortage on the general economic situation and interest rates" was a Keynesian analysis. Our conclusion was that in the short run there would be excess demand, compared with a lower level of supply, but subsequently inadequate demand would appear in the latter part of 1974. This continues to be our general assessment of the situation.' (p. 1)

April 1974 – 'Financial Assessment after the Budget' (see Section 2.8, p. 11)

'A balanced judgement on the budget and its influence on economic activity and financial markets would gain immeasurably from an exercise in marrying the economic forecast of the Treasury with a flows of funds analysis ... The Treasury makes virtually no adjustment to its main economic forecast for the results of the financial forecast ... The Treasury's real terms forecast is that between the second half of 1973 and the second half of 1974 G.D.P. will rise by 21/2 per cent. This is less than the underlying growth of productive capacity of about 3 per cent. By implication, the Treasury is forecasting a modest rise in unemployment. This year's financial forecast, however, is far from being consistent; indeed the discrepancy is so wide that the initial snap judgement of mild deflationary budget arithmetic must give way to a forecast of a deepening recession in the absence of further government action.' (p. 1)

April 1974 – Bulletin, no. 23

'The deflationary impact on domestic economic activity of the increased price of oil is similar to a £2000m. increase in VAT. In addition ... the public sector's underlying borrowing requirement is expected to decrease by some £2000m. in 1974/5. Their combined effect is a change of £4000m. This is a very substantial deflationary force. This conclusion confirms the view expressed in our "Financial assessment after the budget" in which we forecast a deepening recession in the absence of further government action.' (p. 6)

May 1974 – Bulletin, no. 24

'... The implication is that industrial and commercial companies will be forced into very substantial deficit.' (p. 1)
    'One of the ways in which industrial and commercial companies react when forced into financial deficit is to attempt to restore their financial position by reducing capital formation and stock building.' (p. 1)
    '...the substantial deficit of industrial and commercial companies being forecast for 1974/5 implies further downward pressure on ordinary share prices.' (p. 6)

A.9.1.4   Prediction of the Sterling Crisis in October 1976

April 1976 – Bulletin, no. 52, Reprinted in The Guardian, 14 May 1976[1]

'The most important single objective of U.K. economic policy should be to avoid another acceleration of inflation following the business upswing that has just started. There is acute danger that in due course inflation could rise even higher, indeed much higher, than in 1974. The mistakes during the last upswing must be avoided.' (p. 1)

'Although last year's PSFD [public sector financial deficit] was perhaps excusable a PSFD of the same size this year is completely inappropriate now that the economy has started to recover. The error of March 1972 is being repeated. Not only has the lesson not been learnt but the mistake is considerably worse ... (p. 3)

'If no action is taken to neutralise the excess pressures, some combination of the following will tend to occur:

(a) Inflation will be much higher than it would otherwise be ...
(b) Real economic growth will accelerate, but because of inertia this may take some time.
(c) The balance of payments will be much worse than it would otherwise be ...
(d) There will be some short lived speculation in financial assets. In the last cycle it was in property. It will almost certainly be different in this cycle ...' (p. 4)

June 1976 – Bulletin, no. 54

'On Monday 7th June ... the Chancellor stated that there was no "economic justification" for the fall in sterling which has taken place in recent weeks. Mr Healey also stated that there had been no economic justification for the high price of sterling in March 1975. The Chancellor is wrong. He is focusing solely on the competitiveness of British goods and services at a given exchange rate, totally ignoring the other elements of the balance of payments. The monetary approach to the balance of payments, which deals not only with the current account but also with investment and other currency flows, explains the behaviour of sterling. This *Bulletin* shows that an important cause of the outflow of sterling is excessive growth of DCE [domestic credit expansion]. The cause of the growth of DCE is the Government's refusal to cut the budget deficit.' (p. 1)

'... The essence of the monetary approach is that if the domestic supply of money exceeds the domestic demand for money, some of the excess will tend to flow abroad – under a fixed exchange rates the foreign exchange reserves will fall while under floating exchange rates sterling will decline sharply.' (p. 1)

'... In order to determine whether the domestic supply of money is adequate or inadequate, DCE can be compared with the percentage increase in GDP in money terms.' (p. 2)

'...during the three months to mid-May ... DCE was probably about £2250m., an annual growth of 23 per cent p.a. of the money stock ...' (p. 7)

A.9.1.5   Incorrect Prediction in 1977 of Recession After the IMF Measures

November 1976 – 'Why It May Become Necessary to Prevent the Money Supply Rising Too Slowly', Article in The Times, 15 November

'Monetarists agree with neo-Keynesians that cuts in public expenditure contract economic activity *if the money supply is allowed to fall as a result of the lower budget deficit.*' (p. 2)

'The outlook facing the UK is that before many months have passed a new recession will most likely be gathering momentum. The IMF will rightly impose constraints on the UK that public expenditure and the budget deficit must both fall ... the stance of neo-Keynesian fiscal policy *will* be progressively less stimulating ... In these circumstances the money supply will tend substantially to undershoot the 10 per cent target ... the authorities must be ready and aggressively determined to keep the money supply expanding next year right up to the 10 per cent target, if necessary by actually buying in existing long term government debt.' (p. 4)

March 1977, Bulletin, no. 63

'Many people are under the impression that monetary policy has been eased recently because nominal interest rates have been falling ... In the 1950s and 1960s the stance of monetary policy was usually measured by the behaviour of nominal interest rates ... most neo-Keynesians have conceded that the best available measure of the stance of monetary policy is the behaviour of the monetary aggregates ... The current behaviour of the monetary aggregates indicates that, although the authorities have attempted to ease monetary policy, it has in fact been extremely tight. An intense monetary squeeze started in mid-September.' (p. 1)

'In our last two *Bulletins* we have been warning of the danger of the monetary authorities repeating the mistakes made in 1974 ... when they squeezed the money supply too tightly as the economy started to slide into recession ... Is there now sufficient evidence to state that the same mistake has definitely been made again?' (p. 1)

'The main conclusion ... is that the recession will deepen in the second half of this year.' (p. 7)

August 1977 – Bulletin, no. 69

'The battle between the foreign exchange and gilt-edged markets' – It is important to realise why the recent inflow of funds started. A monetary squeeze in real terms is government policy ... In a closed economy, such as the US, the adjustment process tends to be a decline in real growth. In an open economy, such as the UK, a rapid effect ... is the tendency for the exchange rate to appreciate, which helps to reduce inflation quickly. Sterling's present strength is a direct reflection of the recent monetary squeeze.' (p. 3)

'Summarising, the sequence of events has been as follows. A domestic monetary squeeze caused an inflow of funds across the exchanges. The inflow then gathered a momentum of its own.' (p. 4)

'The £522m growth of sterling M3 in the month to mid-July masks massive offsetting flows. External and foreign currency finance increased sterling M3 by no less than £965m but the PSBR less purchases of public sector debt by the non-bank private sector reduced sterling M3 by £679m. This is a dramatic illustration of the forces discussed earlier.' (p. 7)

October 1977 – Bulletin, no. 71

'The intense monetary squeeze in real terms lasted only for six months, from September 1976 to March 1977. This is probably the minimum duration for there to be a significant impact on economic activity. But in March a mild squeeze in real terms appeared likely to continue for many months. This was because the upper limit of the target for monetary growth in nominal terms was (and still is) 13 per cent and the level of inflation, which was then running at about 23 per cent, was expected to decline only slowly. In the event, monetary growth in nominal terms has been close to the top of its target range and inflation has declined rapidly to about 10 per cent. In short, the monetary squeeze in real terms lasted only another three months; it finished in June – much sooner than we had expected.' (p. 1)

'The conclusion of this discussion about the outlook for economic activity is not clear cut. As we stated at the beginning of this *Bulletin*, there is no previous practical experience of a situation similar to that current in the UK Until recently we have been at the most pessimistic end of the range of forecasts of UK economic activity. We are now more optimistic because real monetary growth is no longer being squeezed. The tendency for the recession to feed on itself is most probably being arrested.' (p. 4)

A.9.1.6   Predictions of the 1979–80 Inflation

April 1978 – Bulletin, no. 77

'In recent *Bulletins* we have expressed our growing concern about excessive monetary growth, particularly about the behaviour of M1, but in a somewhat muted fashion ... Our fears are expressed fully in this *Bulletin*.

'We have repeatedly argued in these *Bulletins* that short run aberrations in monetary growth should be ignored. Except under extreme conditions, variations in monetary growth which reverse within about six months have no economic significance. This is why at times these *Bulletins* have been comparatively relaxed about excessive growth. This is not the case at present.' (p. 1)

May 1978 – Bulletin, no. 79

'Given previous excesses, recent monetary data are very disturbing. In terms of analysis, there is little we can add to our last two *Bulletins*. In terms of description, we can express our views more strongly ...' (p. 1)

October 1978 – 'The World Economy', Talk at an International Seminar Held at Gleneagles

'Dollars have poured out of the US into other countries. At first this did no harm; rather it was beneficial. In many countries, domestic monetary growth was inadequate and money flowing in from abroad helped to make good the deficiency. It was an important factor helping to stabilise the world recession.

'But the inflow of money from the US continued. Many countries have short-term buffers which are quite efficient for a few months, to prevent an inflow of money from abroad unduly increasing the growth of their domestic money stock. For example, in the UK our gilt-edged market efficiently neutralised the inflow of funds from abroad until the autumn of 1977. But the absorption of the buffers was soon used up. Starting about a year ago, monetary growth became excessive in most countries of OECD, for example, Germany, Switzerland, Japan, the UK and Italy.' (p. 5)

'... Assume for the moment that I am right that there is excessive monetary growth in OECD. What would you expect to happen? The first thing you would expect is for the price of all existing financial assets to rise. This has been happening ...' (p. 6)

'The next thing you would expect to happen is for price inflation to start to increase ...' (p. 6)

'The third thing one would expect is for real economic growth to start to accelerate ...' (p. 6)

'Earlier, when I was discussing the devaluation of the US dollar, I posed the question of whether primary producers have yet to price in Smithsonian terms (a basket of currencies) rather than in dollars. Markets must first be capable of bearing price increases. The gathering pace of the convoy of the rest of the world and a delay to the expected downturn of the US economy would create the background conditions for this to happen. Speculation in commodities is also a likely result of excessive monetary growth ... This may be the start of a major rise in commodity prices. In 1973 there was a sharp rise. To many industrialised nations this came as a bolt out of the blue. They thought of it as an act of God, for which they were not responsible. The same process is starting to happen again ...' (p. 7)

A.9.1.7 Predictions of the 1979–81 Recession

August 1979 – Article in The Observer, 12 August (see Note 9 of Chapter 3, p. 198)

'It may surprise some people to read that a person with my reputation is worried about the prospect of the money supply rising too slowly ... Most monetary and financial economists argue just as strongly against inadequate monetary growth as they do against excessive monetary growth ... A good example ... was inadequate monetary growth in 1969–70. The same thing occurred in 1974–75. On both occasions Britain subsequently paid the price in a stream of unnecessary bankruptcies and higher unemployment ... Unhappily a replay in 1980 is threatened. A recession seems almost certain to start soon ... I should stress that inadequate monetary growth is not our problem at the moment ... but inadequate growth will be a danger by next year.'

August 1979 – Bulletin, no. 95

'There is no doubt that the financial deficit of industrial and commercial companies is in the process of rising sharply ... the financial deficit could equal or even exceed the worst of 1974/5 ...' (p. 1)

May 1980 – Bulletin, no. 105

'The financial pressure on the corporate sector is becoming progressively tighter ... the monetary squeeze in real terms is now of a similar order to that in mid-1974 ...' (p. 1)

'The behaviour of sterling M3 is not the only indicator of the current tightness of monetary policy. Both the narrower and broader definitions of the money supply confirm the squeeze ... the squeeze in real terms is extremely severe. It is, in fact, more severe than that in 1974, as shown in Table 9.1, below.' (p. 2)

Table 9.1   Real monetary growth (from Greenwell's *Monetary Bulletin*, May 1980)

	At mid-April 1980			At mid-July 1974		
	3 months	*6 months*	*1 year*	*3 months*	*6 months*	*1 year*
Notes & coin	–17% p.a.	–14% p.a.	–12%	–8% p.a.	–8% p.a.	–8%
Retail M1	–24% p.a.	–24% p.a.	–18%	–15% p.a.	–13% p.a.	–17%
Sterling M3	–18% p.a.	–14% p.a.	–11%	–15% p.a.	–12% p.a.	–1%
M4	–17% p.a.	–14% p.a.	–9%	n.a.	n.a.	n.a.
M5	–15% p.a.	–12% p.a.	–9%	n.a.	n.a.	n.a.

Note: Data in 1974 are for M1 because those for retail M1 are not available. [Retail M1 is M1 less wholesale overnight interest-bearing deposits.]

June 1980 – Bulletin, no. 106 (see Note 9 of Chapter 3, p. 198)

'Last month it seemed possible that the government was drifting into a most dangerous type of monetary policy. The following types of tight policy can be distinguished:
  (i)   gradualism
 (ii)   shock treatment and
(iii)   sustained pressure significantly more severe than gradualists advocate.' (p. 2)
    '... The third type of policy, namely sustained pressure significantly more severe than the gradualists advocate, runs the greatest chance of an enforced U-turn. The monetary pressure involved is neither restricted to a level deemed to be safe [as with gradualism] nor is it of strictly limited duration [as with shock treatment].' (p. 3)

A.9.1.8   Unfounded Worries About Inflation in the Early 1980s

January 1981 – Bulletin, no. 114

'This *Bulletin* argues that:
  (i)   the excess growth in sterling M3 over the last eight months should not be allowed to stay in the system,
 (ii)   the excess is likely to take longer than usual to work through into prices and, therefore, there is still time for the authorities to mop it up,
(iii)   the excess is being held by the personal sector and arises from the increase in the savings ratio, and
(iv)   the most pressing monetary problem is to persuade the personal sector to save in a less liquid form ...' (p. 1)

February 1981 – Bulletin, no. 115

'The analysis of the monetary situation in the U.K. is once again intensely controversial. This is partly the familiar question of how relaxed or severe monetary policy should be. Increasingly, however, it is a question of how severe the present monetary policy actually is. This debate is not about fine detail, of interest only to experts. It is of practical importance. The recent *Annual Monetary Review* of the City University Business School, for example, contains an assessment that the recent stance of monetary policy has been very easy and that, as a consequence, inflation will rise to 16 per cent in 1982.

'On the surface, virtually all the indicators, whether economic, financial or monetary, are consistent with the proposition that the monetary squeeze is severe ...' (p. 1)

'Much more relevant is the behaviour of the narrower monetary measures ...' (p. 1)

'During the last year in the U.K., the behaviour of both the monetary base and narrow money has been very different from that of broad money. More precisely, the growth of sterling M3 (and of PSL1 and PSL2) since last April has clearly been excessive, whilst that of M1 (and of Retail M1) has been sluggish. Further, the growth of the monetary base, as usually measured, has been declining steadily for as long as two and a half years, from an annual rate of 18 per cent to one of about 6 per cent.' (p. 1)

'We have three conclusions. Firstly, for as long as the authorities retain their present system of monetary control, we consider that it is unwise to judge the stance of monetary policy from the behaviour of the narrow monetary measures. It is important to look at all the monetary indicators, and not just some of them ...' (p. 5)

'Secondly, a rise in inflation to 16 per cent in 1982, as forecast by the City University, is not yet inevitable ... The excess of broad money will not have harmful effects as long as the growth of the monetary base continues to be sluggish ...' (p. 5)

'Thirdly, during the last two and a half years, the rate of growth of the monetary base has declined steadily, almost exactly in line with the gradualist path advocated by most monetarists. If anything the path has been steeper than many would have risked. If the authorities could ensure that the decline continued, they could ignore all the other monetary indicators, including the current excessive growth of broad money ...' (p. 5)

'In the absence of an efficient system of monetary control, the only prudent course of action at present open to the authorities is to mop up the current excess of liquidity in the private sector. The fact is that the present system of control is inefficient and we cannot rely on the monetary base continuing to behave in a desirable way.' (p. 5)

March 1981 – 'The Budget', Bulletin, no. 116[2]

'The expansion of the broader aggregates since the middle of 1980 has clearly not been due to buoyant demand. GDP at market prices has not been expanding rapidly, since both activity in real terms and price inflation have been falling. The expansion has, instead, been the result of the buoyant supply. This has come from the increase in personal savings; the ratio of savings to personal disposable income reached a record 17 per cent in the third quarter of 1980 compared with 13 per cent in 1979 as a whole. The additional savings have been held initially in a highly liquid form, which is the reason why the PSL [private sector liquidity] series have been buoyant.' (p. 4)

'When the reason for excessive monetary growth is buoyant demand for money, the appropriate response is to increase interest rates. When the reason is buoyancy savings, the appropriate response is to encourage people to save in a less liquid form.' (p. 4)

'Overall, our view is that the money supply may well return to a desirable path; indeed, it may tend to go too far. In our introduction we implied that the intended tightening of fiscal policy might be excessive ... the tightening of fiscal policy together with the measures discussed above may lead the behaviour of the broader measures of the money supply to swing from one extreme to the other.' (p. 5)

'At various times in the past, we have warned of the dangers of monetary policy being allowed to become too tight. The warnings in January 1974, November 1976 and August 1979 were all given about six months before the event. On each occasion, they gave rise to some scepticism because the current problem was still excessive monetary growth.' (p. 5)

'Our feeling is that another such warning may now be appropriate even though the recent growth of the broad aggregates has been excessive. With the current recession so deep, and with fiscal policy having been tightened, it is most important that the monetary squeeze should not be allowed to become too acute in the coming months. Assessing the acuteness will be a matter of fine judgement at the time.' (p. 5)

July 1986 – 'Why Those Inflation Fears Are Baseless', article in The Times, 18 July

'... I have found it useful to pay most attention to ... M0, non-interest bearing M1 and M2. These have suggested that the stance of policy has been about right. In the last few months, however, their growth has accelerated slightly. In my judgement monetary policy has been relaxed a little but this seems appropriate given the continuing rise in unemployment and the fall in inflation.

'... circumstances could change in a way which would arouse anxiety if the growth of sterling M3 does not at the same time contract. For instance, if short-term rates fall relative to long-term rates, bank deposits will no longer be such an excellent home for savings. In this new circumstance the current level of bank deposits would be dangerously high.'

A.9.1.9 Predictions of the 1989–90 Inflation

August 1987 – 'Alarm Bells', Bulletin, no. 192 (see Section 3.6, p. 25)

'Introduction:
For the first time since Mrs Thatcher became Prime Minister the behaviour of the money supply is beginning to give serious cause for concern; the alarm bells are starting to ring ...' (p. 1)

'Until the middle of 1986 ... the buoyancy of M3 was for savings purposes and was not a cause for concern. The situation started to change in the middle of 1986. The alteration was not in the growth of M3, which remained very high, but in non-interest bearing M1, which accelerated ... and in relative interest rates. The growth in transactions demand started to be an important reason for the buoyancy of M3, and bank deposits lost a lot of their attraction as a savings medium relative to alternative investments.

'The situation in the second half of 1986 warranted very close monitoring. Initially this provided reassurance. The six and three month growth rates suggested that M3 was decelerating last winter; the confirming patterns in M4 and M5 were even more marked. The published data for the narrow aggregates also displayed some deceleration early this year, although it was less clear and could be explained by distortions.

'Hopes of deceleration were in the event nullified by the publication of buoyant monetary data for the month of May. The preliminary data for June were also buoyant.

'The conclusion is that the grounds for disregarding the buoyancy of M3 which were in force in 1980 and 1985/6 are not valid in current circumstances. The authorities should be taking steps to reduce money supply growth.' (p. 6)
'Conclusions:
'... For the first time since Mrs Thatcher became Prime Minister data for the money supply suggest that it is appropriate to start sounding the alarm bells.' (p. 7)

A.9.1.10   Predictions of the 1987 Stock Market Crash

September 1987 – Bulletin, no. 193

'Surplus money can be spent in four ways ... the money can be spent on domestic assets, in which case stock-market and property prices will tend to rise. (p. 3)

'The overall effect is inflationary, as it was in 1972/5, but the crucial difference this time is that the prices which have been rising are not those of goods and services but those of assets, for example ordinary shares.' (p. 4)

'If financial forces are responsible for a rise in a market there is a danger that a speculative bubble can form and that the market will subsequently crash when the bubble bursts, as it will almost certainly do at some stage ...'[3] (p. 5)

'The first part of this *Bulletin* has described the mechanism for the formation of a bubble in a capital market. Given the [current] behaviour of the money and credit aggregates it would be no surprise whatsoever if a bubble existed in the equity market. Indeed it would be surprising if one did not exist ...' (p. 15)

'The conclusion is that the market is dangerously overvalued by UK historical standards. This is powerful evidence confirming the bubble.' (p. 15)

A.9.1.11   'Wobble' After the Stock Market Crash in October 1987

October 1987 – Bulletin, no. 194

'Where do we go from here? Although a deterioration in the outlook for dividends, earnings and profits was not the cause of the fall in the equity markets, the sharp fall in share prices will have a substantial contractionary impact on economic activity ... The danger facing world economies has changed from inflation back to recession ... The greatest danger is the US.' (p. 4)

December 1987 – Bulletin, no. 196

'In the immediate future there will be a battle between two powerful opposing forces. The deflationary force is the reduction in wealth and the loss of confidence, particularly in the US, arising from the fall in equity markets. The expansionary force is not merely the modest recent reductions in interest rates; the injection of liquidity arising from the massive central bank intervention [in foreign exchange markets] is likely to be more powerful.

'Neither the expansionary nor the contractionary forces can be quantified, let alone the difference between them. One cannot be dogmatic about which will be the more powerful, at any rate in the short run.' (p. 4)

January 1988 – 'US Recession Inevitable', article in The Times, 25 July

'The behaviour of the money supply in the US has a dramatic message for economies and markets. An American recession seems inevitable. The only question is how soon will it start.'

January 1988 – Bulletin, no. 197

'The conclusion from this line of argument is that the underlying reason for the US economy's lack of response [to stimulatory measures] in the 1930's was that it had become "loaned up". After so many years of financial promiscuity a severe recession had almost certainly become unavoidable.' (p. 5)
'Conclusion:
'The parallel between events in the US in the 1920s and those in the 1980s appears too close for comfort. The outcome this time may be that the US economy will muddle through with a recession of typical postwar size. There is nevertheless a distinct possibility of something much more serious.' (p. 5)

February 1988 – Talk Given at a Conference Organised by The Economist and NEDO, London

'In conclusion, there is a definite risk that the US economy will experience a recession substantially deeper than a typical post war recession. But this is not a central forecast. The most likely outcome may well be that the US will muddle through with a recession of normal depth but there is, say, one chance in four of real trouble.' (p. 9)

April 1988 – Gilt-edged Market Background, 5 April[4]

'The general picture is of monetary deceleration prior to the budget. If it were not for the Budget's boost to confidence, we would be expecting the economy to slow. As it is, there are no clear conclusions.' (p. 4)

April 1988[5] – 'Will Inflation Follow Rapid Monetary Growth?', Article in Economic Affairs, June/July Edition

'At the time of writing this article in April, the economy appears to be growing at well over 4 per cent per annum which is very rapid by past UK standards. The fall in the stock market in October has not damped it as expected ... It is nevertheless clear that there is some overheating ... The overheating is caused by excessive monetary growth and the main reason for this is very buoyant bank lending to individuals ...' (p. 6)

'The most recently published monetary indicators for the UK suggest that the economy was probably decelerating slightly on the eve of the Budget. The six month rate of growth of M0 fell from 8.5 per cent per annum at the end of December to 4.5 per cent at the end of February. That for M4, which is now the government's preferred definition of broad money, fell from 17 per cent per annum to just over 13 per cent per annum. The Budget has, however, given a boost to confidence. This is likely to encourage more borrowing and, therefore, the deceleration may cease. There is no evidence giving one confidence that the current overheating will wane of its own accord ...' (p. 7)

'The authorities are currently ignoring excessive monetary growth which is not caused by the public sector. They used to take countervailing action if M3 was growing too rapidly because of buoyant bank lending; they increased their sales of gilt-edged stock. In October 1985 the Chancellor announced the suspension of this policy of "overfunding". The suspension was right in the circumstances but these have now changed.' (p. 8)[6]

A.9.1.12   *Predictions of the 1990–2 Recession*

November 1988 – 'Market Crashes, Deflation and Long Waves', Bulletin, no. 200

'One thing is certain – history [comparison with 1929 and the 1930s] never repeats itself exactly – there are always major variations on the theme. The most important variation this time will occur because central banks are aware that the money supply should be controlled. Stopping the money supply from falling should prevent a general fall in prices. The second of Irving Fisher's two conditions should not, therefore, be present.' (p. 6)

'Controlling the money supply will not, however, stop a fall in the price of particular assets, and this can easily lead to an asset deficiency rather than a liquidity problem in the sector affected. Once the market has detected the existence of an asset deficiency, pumping in money and liquidity has little direct effect. For example, the huge increase in liquidity outside the US in 1987, resulting from the Louvre Accord intervention to support the dollar, did not help the LDC debt situation. Currently, an increase in the money supply in the US would do very little to restore the financial position of US savings and loans organisations.' (p. 6)

'Nasty cases of financial embarrassment are, therefore, likely but they will, in all probability, be contained by government action, as with US savings and loans organisations. It should be possible to prevent major chain reactions.' (p. 6)

'Conclusions:

'It is the variations on themes which catch forecasters out. It is wise to confine predictions to aspects which are reasonably clear. My first forecast is that in due course Japan will experience its version of October 1987 in the US. Let us hope that Japanese discipline holds and that a downward adjustment in valuation can be managed in an orderly way.

'My second forecast is that the downward trend of interest rates is intact. The second half of the bull market in bonds of a life time will eventually occur and this time interest rates will fall in real as well as in nominal terms.

'Finally, talk of 1929, depression and market crashes conveys extreme gloom but remember the variation on the theme. Having said that, I will not personally relax until the valuation of Japanese assets seems more secure, the adverse trend in US balance sheets has started to reverse, and real interest rates have fallen. The last will be the clearest signal. Whilst real interest rates remain historically so high, economies are battling against the remorseless power of compound interest.' (p. 7)

January 1991 – 'The Dangers of World Debt Deflation', Article in the Financial Times, 16 January

'In conclusion, there are parallels between the present state of the world's credit markets and the debt deflation of the 1920s and 1930s. The great difference is that the central banks should have learnt the lesson that the money supply must not be allowed to contract whatever happens.'

February 1991 – Letter from the 'Liverpool Six' to The Times, 13 February

The Liverpool Six consisted of Tim Congdon, Bill Martin, Patrick Minford, Alan Walters, Peter Warburton and the author, see Section 10.2, p. 160.

'We are deeply concerned about the state of the economy. The principles of good monetary policy imply that interest rates should have been cut significantly by now in response to the clear evidence of recession from the monetary and indeed all other indicators.

'Failure to cut them is increasing the risks of a depression which would get out of control and from which recovery would be long delayed.'

January 1992 – Letter from the Liverpool Six to The Times, 7 January

'As in our letter to you published on February 13, 1991, we continue to be deeply concerned about the state of the economy ... On present policies there is a serious risk that national output, which probably declined by 2.5 percent in 1991, will keep falling in early 1992. The current recession will probably be the longest in the post war period and it may also prove the deepest.'

July 1992 – Letter from the Liverpool Six to The Times, 14 July

'Just as real interest rates were driven too low in 1987 and 1988 in order to keep the pound down, so in the past couple of years they have been held too high in order to keep the pound up, at an overvalued rate. The weakening state of the banking system, the collapse of credit, and the liquidity drain created by huge sales of government stock now add to the serious risk that the present slump of which we warned will be deepened and prolonged well into 1993 and beyond.'

February 1993 – 'A Policy for Debt Deflation', Economic Viewpoint, Economic Outlook, London Business School

'The final stages of debt-deflation are most unlikely to occur in the UK. The authorities will not allow a major bank to fail: depositors will not lose their money. It is also most unlikely that banks will have to call in loans because they have insufficient capital.

'The worst threat in the UK is that banks may have insufficient capital to supply credit to new borrowers but even this appears unlikely.

'The probable threat is that when the economy starts to recover and firms need additional credit to finance a rise in work-in-progress, etc., banks will consider that much of the demand comes from applicants who are not creditworthy.' (p. 36)

PART III

Refinements, Further Evidence and Policy Implications

10 The 'Liverpool Six'

The record of monetarist forecasts given in the last chapter included three letters from the 'Liverpool Six' to *The Times*. The six were Tim Congdon of Gerrard & National/Lombard Street Research, Bill Martin of UBS Philips & Drew, Patrick Minford of Liverpool University, Alan Walters, who had returned to Washington, Peter Warburton of Robert Fleming, and the author. The six were a spin-off from the Shadow Monetary Policy Group.

10.1 THE SHADOW MONETARY POLICY GROUP

After Nigel Lawson resigned as Chancellor of the Exchequer in October 1989 and Alan Walters had returned to Washington, John Major became the new Chancellor and the influence of monetarists waned because, as far as was known, he did not have any outside advisers. This was not surprising, because the press would have had a field-day if they had caught the new Chancellor with an adviser following the witch-hunt of Alan Walters.[1]

Partly in response to the loss of influence, the Shadow Monetary Policy Group was founded in May 1990, under the auspices of the Institute of Economic Affairs, whose director, Graham Mather, was chairman. The secretary was Robert Miller, who was also closely associated with the IEA.[2] The group was meant to be modelled on the Shadow Open Market Committee in the US but the members, who were a combination of City economists and academics, would not all have described themselves as monetarists. The members were Giles Keating of Credit Suisse First Boston, Peter Spencer of Shearson Lehman and Geoffrey Wood of City University Business School, together with Tim Congdon, Bill Martin, Patrick Minford, Alan Walters, and the author. The group met every three months or so and issued bulletins about the conduct of monetary policy.

It soon became apparent that there were various tensions within the group. The one that exploded in public was about the merits of the UK being a member of the Exchange Rate Mechanism (ERM) of the European Monetary System. Matters came to a head when Patrick Minford took the initiative and five of the members, plus Peter Warburton, clubbed together to write the first of the letters to *The Times*. The letter was reported on the front page of that newspaper and attracted considerable publicity. The authors were subsequently dubbed the Liverpool Six by the media. Graham Mather disagreed strongly with the views expressed and said so in public, and a row ensued.[3]

10.2   THE LIVERPOOL SIX

After the dust had settled the Liverpool Six met independently of the IEA. The six members were in full agreement about ERM but not about everything else. An initial objective was to find out the extent to which agreement could be reached. This was thought important because any further public disagreement amongst monetarists would continue to undermine confidence in monetarism.

The most important area of disagreement was about the relative importance of narrow and broad money. This was the dispute, referred to in Chapter 4, that had helped to bring monetarism into disrepute in the 1980s. Patrick Minford believed that the focus should be on narrow money, especially M0. Tim Congdon believed that the behaviour of narrow money had no significance whatsoever and concentrated entirely on broad money, at first on sterling M3 and later on M4. (M4 includes building society deposits; attention switched after building societies were allowed to compete with banks and deposits with them became similar). The author spent some time trying to act as elder statesman and mediate between Minford and Congdon. The result was a considerable narrowing of the gap, but not sufficiently for the Liverpool Six, or a reformed Shadow Monetary Policy Group, to continue with a high profile.

The outcome of the attempt to mediate was very positive as far as the author's own thinking was concerned, because it clarified many of the issues. The next chapter has benefited greatly as a result. The author has already described how he is a great picker of other people's brains and he certainly owes a debt to both Tim Congdon and Patrick Minford.

11 The Current State of Knowledge

This chapter contains the conclusions from the author's observation over the years of the workings of the monetary system, the characteristics of the different monetary aggregates and what he has learnt about forecasting techniques.

11.1 THE USE OF M0 AND M1 AS INDICATORS

The narrowest of the monetary aggregates (that is, notes and coin in circulation with the public, cash held by banks and banks' balances with the Bank) has two names – M0 and monetary base. Some monetarists, including the author, advocate that the central bank should control the supply of this aggregate directly and the term monetary base is usually used in this context (see Pepper 1993). It is important to draw a distinction between such control of the monetary base and the use of the aggregate merely as an indicator. The term M0 is usually used in the latter context. This section is about M0's use as an indicator.

M0's characteristics depend crucially on whether or not the monetary base is being controlled. If it is not, as is the case currently in the UK, M0 is determined mainly by the demand for it and not by its supply, as would be the case if the monetary base where controlled directly. Under the UK's current system causality runs mainly from the economy to M0, and not the other way round as would be the case if the base where controlled. Failure to appreciate this has lead to much confusion.

Because M0 is largely demand-determined it might be thought that it would be merely a coincidental indicator of the UK economy but this is not so. M0's largest component is notes and coin in circulation with the public and, as a result, M0 is influenced mainly by the behaviour of retail sales. Retail sales are, in turn, a leading indicator of the economy in the sense that if they grow at an unsustainable rate there will be inflation or a problem with the balance of payments, or both. M0 is, therefore, also a leading indicator.

There is a growing amount of statistical evidence that the lead of M0 is more than merely a reflection of retail sales. Tim Congdon is not convinced that this is so and extends his analysis to other measures of narrow money. He argues that if someone's holdings of notes and coin do not coincide with the desired level, then most people merely transfer funds to or from their current accounts (demand accounts in US terminology) (see Congdon 1992a, 1992b). More generally, current accounts are also demand-determined, because people can transfer money to or from deposit accounts (time deposits). Under the UK's system of control such transfers between one type of money and another have no effect on the economy.

There are, however, a small number of people who do not have an account with either a bank or a building society. Others do not have a deposit account as well as a current account. Even if they do, probably only a few have arrangements with their banks to transfer funds automatically between accounts to maintain a constant balance on their current account. If they do not have such an arrangement they have to make a conscious decision to transfer money from their deposit account to their current account when the balance on the latter falls below the desired level. They may well take the need to make such a transfer as an indication that they are overspending. Small businesses, in particular, pay great attention to monitoring cash flow. As well as making a transfer from a deposit account, people may decide to cut back on expenditure, with consequential effects on the economy.

More generally, one of the essential roles of money, already mentioned, is to act as a buffer bridging the interval of time between expenditure being incurred and income being received in an uncertain world. This applies to narrow as well as broad money. The level of money that an individual holds is often different from the ultimately desired balance. It will be larger if income is either higher or has been received sooner than expected, or if expenditure has been delayed or is lower than expected. Conversely, it will be lower if expenditure has occurred sooner than expected or if income has been delayed, etc. The person will subsequently take action to restore his money balance to the desired level. At any point of time many people will be in the process of adjusting their monetary positions towards their desired balance. There are lags in the adjustment process and whilst they are taking place narrow money is partly supply-determined. The same applies to some extent to M0.

The above argument does not imply that changes in narrow money or M0 *cause* changes in expenditure. Narrow money is merely behaving as a pressure gauge. A barometer, for example, reflects a phenomenon that precedes bad weather; it does not cause the weather. One statistic can be a leading indicator of another without there being a causal relationship between the two.

11.1.1 Non-interest-bearing M1

The author has found non-interest-bearing M1 (nibM1) of key importance on some occasions. Its usefulness depends on the direction in which interest rates are changing.

If interest rates are rising, people tend to economise on their holdings of money that do not earn interest. People transfer some of their balances in non-interest-bearing current accounts into accounts on which interest is paid. The result is that the impact of a rise in interest rates on nibM1 is usually greater, and is certainly quicker, than the effect of the rise in rates on economic activity. Growth of nibM1 can accordingly become sluggish whilst the economy continues to boom. Sluggish growth of M1 after interest rates have been raised may *not* indicate that monetary policy has been tightened sufficiently. *It can provide false reassurance*. This was a lesson from the Heath–Barber boom of 1972–3. At the opposite phase of the business cycle buoyant growth of M1 when interest rates are falling does not necessarily indicate that monetary policy has been eased sufficiently and that a recession will end.

NibM1 is a useful indicator when its growth is buoyant in spite of interest rates rising and when its growth is sluggish in spite of interest rates falling. The former is a definite indication that policy has not been tightened sufficiently, as in 1986 and especially in early 1987, which provided a clear signal of the inflation that was to come. Sluggish growth of nibM1 when interest rates are falling is a definite signal that a recession is likely to continue, as happened in the first half of 1980.

11.1.2 Conclusions About Narrow Money

The general conclusion about narrow money – in particular about non-interest-bearing money – is that it is useful as a negative indicator, that is, that something is not happening, rather than as a positive indicator that something is happening. The behaviour of narrow money can indicate that policy has not been eased, or tightened, sufficiently but not that sufficient action has been taken. Put in another way, a change in the rate of growth of narrow money is a necessary but not a sufficient condition for an economic turning point to occur.

11.2   THE USE OF BROAD MONEY FOR FORECASTING

The crucial difference between broad and narrow money is that changes in broad money, and liquidity, can *cause* changes in economic activity and inflation.

The first point to make is that the supply of broad money is not always equal to the demand for it; that is, the market in money may not be in equilibrium. This point is disputed by some monetarists, for example by Patrick Minford, but close observation of the financial scene indicates that imbalances between supply and demand do in fact occur (see Pepper 1994: ch. 15).

If the supply of broad money is in surplus, the excess money can be spent in four ways:
  (i)   on goods and services, in which case economic activity accelerates,
  (ii) in a way that directly raises the price of goods and services, for example on a commodity, in which case inflation rises,
  (iii) on non-sterling assets, for example sterling deposits may be exchanged for dollar ones, in which case sterling tends to fall, and
  (iv) on domestic assets, in which case stock-market and property prices tend to rise and the change in wealth in due course affects economic activity.

This section is mainly about the first two of the above ways in which money can be spent (see Pepper 1994 for a discussion about the fourth way). The factors determining the supply of money are analysed before those determining the demand for money.

11.2.1   The Supply of Broad Money

The supply of broad money depends in the short run on what is happening in the market for credit. The credit market may well be out of equilibrium, with the demand for finance in the economy as a whole not equal to the supply of saving. When this happens banks act as a buffer; that is, they are the residual source of credit for both government and industry. If the government does not succeed in raising all the finance that it needs in the gilt-edged market and from other non-bank sources, the remainder is automatically borrowed from the banks, at least in the short run. When industry's internal cash flow is inadequate to finance stocks (inventories) and fixed investment, and if industry does not obtain the remainder through the stock market, etc., companies tend to use their overdraft facilities and credit lines with banks. Therefore, when the demand for credit begins to exceed its supply, both industry and government begin to borrow on a large scale from banks.

It should be stressed that banks cannot in the short-run control the total of their holdings of assets because their customers, rather than the banks themselves, determine the take-up of overdraft facilities and credit lines. Banks have also only a little direct influence on the amount that the government borrows from them. (In more detail, the usual result of a bank purchasing gilt-edged stock is a fall in the treasury bill issue and no change in the total of banks' combined holdings of treasury bills and gilt-edged stock. The total will however fall if gilt-edged prices rise as a result of the bank's purchase and this encourages a non-bank to sell stock, in which case the treasury bill issue and banks' holdings of bills will not fall and banks will have increased their lending to the government.)

With customers and the government very largely determining banks' total holdings of assets, banks bid for the necessary funds to finance these holdings. This determines the level of bank deposits and hence the stock of money. (There are however some indirect affects. Relative interest rates will change as banks bid more or less aggressively for funds and this may alter non-banks' desire to hold public-sector assets, the government's residual borrowing from banks and hence the money stock.)

Recapitulating, in the short run changes in the *money stock* depend crucially on imbalances between the supply and demand for *credit* in the economy outside the banking sector. *In this sense*, the *supply* of broad money depends on what is happening in the market for credit.

The level of interest rates has not been mentioned in the above analysis. This may seem surprising in view of the influence of short-term rates on both the supply and demand for credit. The explanation for the omission is that under the UK's system of monetary control the level of short-term rates is not determined by market forces but is administered by the Bank. The demand and supply of credit described above are at the level of interest rates set by the Bank. The Bank may have chosen the equilibrium rate but this is unlikely.

It might be thought that banks bidding for the funds necessary to finance their holdings of assets would bring the demand for money into line with supply. Such reasoning fails to distinguish between the position of banks and that of their customers; it fails to distinguish between what is happening in the money market and the monetary situation in the economy as a whole. This is explained in Appendix 11.1.

11.2.2   The Demand for Broad Money

The factors determining the demand for broad money in the economy as a whole depend on the purposes for which it is held. There are two main ones. Money is held to facilitate transactions and as a medium for savings.

The primary determinant of the demand for money for transactions purposes is the behaviour of national income but the *level* of interest rates on bank deposits also has an influence. As far as the primary determinant is concerned, the demand for money rises both as real economic activity increases and with inflation. The effect of changes in interest rates is a little more complicated. Money for transactions purposes tends to be held in non-interest-bearing or low-interest-bearing deposits, that is, in mainly narrow money. The demand for these falls as interest rates increase as people exchange these deposits for ones on which the full rate of interest is paid, as already explained. The transfers are, however, merely from one sort of deposit to another, from deposits held for transactions purposes to ones held as savings. Broad money is not directly affected, because it includes both types of deposit.

The main determinants of the demand for money for saving purposes are wealth and the merit of bank deposits as an investment relative to the alternatives available. The latter depends on how the rate of interest on bank deposits compares with the expected return on other assets, after taking risk into account. The important factor is *relative interest rates* rather than their *level*.

Summarising, money is held for two main purposes, to facilitate transactions and as a medium for savings. The part that is held for transactions purposes is determined largely by demand. The remainder of the money stock is determined largely by supply. The system is out of equilibrium if the remainder is not equal to the demand for money for savings.

11.2.3   Disequilibrium

Continuing the analysis, any surplus money in the remainder can be:

(i)   unintended savings,
(ii) intended savings but with savers unhappy about the rate of return on bank deposits relative to the expected return available on other investments.

If the deposits are unintended savings, economic activity will rise as they are spent and in due course inflation may rise.

If the deposits are intended savings but savers are unhappy about the return on them, savers will switch out of these deposits into other assets. The result will be asset-price inflation, as distinct from the usual type of inflation which may be called product-price inflation. The rise in asset prices will in due course stimulate the economy, as wealth and confidence rise, and product-price inflation will follow if corrective action is not taken. It should be noted that in the case of savers being unhappy about the return on bank deposits the time lag between monetary growth and the response of economic activity will be longer than usual, as happened in the 1980s.

If savers are happy with the level of bank deposits they are holding as savings, the system will be in equilibrium but only for as long as the pattern of relative expected returns remains unchanged. Any change in relative expected returns will upset the equilibrium, with consequential effects on the economy.

11.2.4 Conclusion About Broad Money

If economic activity is to be forecast successfully from the behaviour of broad money then allowance must be made for changes in relative interest rates and shifts in the demand for money for savings purposes.

11.3 TURNING POINTS

The behaviour of narrow and of broad money at turning points of the economy differ slightly. One of the factors influencing narrow money lengthens the lead of this aggregate, whereas one of those influencing broad money shortens its lead.

Considering narrow money first, a rise in interest rates during an economic upswing has a quicker effect on the growth of non-interest-bearing money than on economic activity, as explained above. Because of this narrow money turns downward sooner than would otherwise be the case, extending its lead over the eventual downturn in economic activity. In the opposite phase of the cycle a fall in interest rates during a recession boosts the growth of non-interest-bearing money sooner than that of the economy. The lead of narrow money over the subsequent economic upswing is again lengthened.

The turning points of broad money in contrast can be delayed by shifts in the savings demand for money, upwards as a boom nears its end and downwards as a recession nears its trough. Although it has been argued that the money stock is supply-determined in the short run, the market tends towards equilibrium in the longer term, with the demand for money exerting some influence on the money stock. One example of this happening is a consequence of the usual inversion of the term structure of interest rates as a boom turning point of the economy approaches. With rates of interest on bank deposits higher than those on longer-term assets, many savers are attracted by the former and prefer bank deposits to gilt-edged stock. As a result non-bank purchases of gilt-edged stock tend to be lower than would otherwise be the case, which means that the money supply is higher. This can delay the slowdown of broad money. At the recession turning point, rates of interest on bank deposits are relatively low, non-bank purchases of gilt-edged stock may be high and this can delay the upswing in broad money.

11.3.1 Conclusions About Turning Points

The overall conclusion is that it is dangerous to base a forecast of a turning point solely on the behaviour of narrow money. It is much safer to wait for confirmation from the behaviour of broad money. The forecaster should then react quickly.

11.4 PRACTICAL POINTS

11.4.1 Assessing the Adequacy of Monetary Growth

Many attempts have been made to establish equations that explain the behaviour of the demand for money, from such things as the growth of the economy, the rate of inflation and the long-run trend in velocity of circulation. An accurate way of assessing whether the supply of money is in surplus or deficit is to calculate the current demand for money using such an equation and compare the result with the actual behaviour of the money stock. A less accurate method is to compare the rate of growth of the money supply with that of GDP, which ignores the long-run trend in the velocity of circulation. An even less accurate method is to focus on monetary growth in real terms, which ignores the current rate of growth of the economy.

In the author's experience, focusing on monetary growth in real terms is usually adequate given the general inaccuracies of the technique because of the variability of the time lag between changes in monetary growth and the response of the economy. Nevertheless the approximation must be born in mind because there are occasions when a more detailed calculation is appropriate. (It should be noted that targets for the money supply should be set in nominal and not real terms, because they can be achieved through higher inflation if they are set in real terms. Similarly, if there is balance of payments problem, the target should be for domestic credit expansion and not the money supply because a target for the latter can be hit by a deterioration in the balance of payments.)

The above argument does not mean that monetary growth in nominal terms should be ignored when making forecasts. The author has always kept an eye on what is happening in nominal terms, because it does appear to have some significance for forecasting. The explanation is probably that changes in monetary growth in nominal terms affect cash flow. The argument is similar to one for interest rates; interest rates that are very high in nominal terms can have a deflationary impact on the economy even if they are low in real terms because cash flow is reduced as borrowers are forced into early repayment of capital.

11.4.2   Time Lags

It has already been stressed that the lags between changes in monetary growth and alterations in GDP are long and variable. Forecasts of the economy would be more accurate if the factors controlling the length of lag were understood and the lags could be predicted.

A word of warning should be given. As has already been mentioned, monetarism is often accused of being like a black box; that is, the transmission mechanism is mysterious and is not explained. Money, like water, will percolate through somewhere and it may not be possible to forecast the location or the length of time before it appears. Further money's essential role as a buffer has been described; the time that a buffer takes to work is nearly always hard to predict. The variability of the time lag between changes in monetary growth and the response of the economy is inherent.

It should be stressed that fluctuations in the money supply that last for less than about six months have no significance for the economy. This interval gives time for things to settle down after any injection, or contraction, has occurred.

Dealing with an injection, the money can be either transactions or savings money. The former will tend to be spent initially on goods and services whereas the latter will tend to be spent on assets. As the deposits change hands the mixture alters, for example savings money may be used to purchase an asset that is being sold by the seller to finance consumption. Each time the money changes hands the composition becomes progressively more normal and the proportion of transactions balances stabilises.

There is a further point. Some of the money that has been injected may not stay in the system for long. Some transactions destroy money, for example some of the money may be used to pay taxes, repay a bank loan or purchase a gilt-edged stock, in which case it will never be spent on goods and services. The wait of six months gives time for such dissipation to occur.

Summarising, if forecasts are to be reliable then conclusions should not be drawn from changes in monetary growth persisting for less than six months.

11.4.3   Momentum

One factor that appears to affect a time lag is momentum in the immediate past. Taking the case of a monetary slowdown, the lag before a recession occurs tends to be longer than usual if the preceding monetary upswing has been large and has lasted for a long time. In these circumstances a reversal of monetary forces takes time to take effect. The surplus money in the system has to be mopped up before the slowdown bites. In Keynesian terms a powerful economic upswing that has been allowed to gather momentum takes time to reverse. Correspondingly the lag tends to be shorter than usual if little momentum has been allowed to build up.

11.4.4   Levels Versus Flows

The focus of attention so far has been on changes in monetary growth rather than on the amount of money in existence, that is on changes in a flow rather than on the level of a stock. It might be thought that the more significant indicator for the economy would be the ratio of the stock of money to GDP; that an abnormally high ratio would be a signal that the economy was likely to grow quickly whereas an abnormally low one would be a warning of recession. In practice it is found that changes in a flow, that is, in monetary growth, are more important. Nevertheless the level of the stock also matters. About three-quarter weight should be given to what is happening to the flow and about one-quarter to the level of the stock. This is roughly consistent with the above discussion about momentum. (The P^* approach is also useful in that it reminds someone scrutinising a flow that the stock position is also relevant.)

11.4.5   The Influence of the Exchange Rate

The time lag may also be influenced by the behaviour of the exchange rate. The lag between a monetary slowdown and a recession tends to be shorter than usual if the exchange rate is allowed to appreciate, because of the consequential squeeze on industrial profits and damage to industrial confidence. In the opposite phase of the cycle the time lag following a monetary upswing tends to be short if the exchange rate is low; the boost to corporate profits encourages an economic upswing.

11.4.6 Corporate Versus Personal Sectors

The corporate and personal sectors react to changes in their money balances differently. The *Monetary Bulletin* in the 1970s and 1980s included analysis of the sectoral flow of funds to try to explain the monetary black box. More recently Tim Congdon has done useful work in this area (see Congdon *Monthly Economic Reviews*).

11.4.7 Financial Versus Spending Counterparts

The components of changes in the money supply can be broken down into ones closely associated with expenditure on goods and services and ones that are financial in nature. An example of the former is a rise in monetary growth that is due to an increase in the PSBR brought about by a rise in government expenditure on goods and services. An example of the latter is monetary growth due to lower sales of gilt-edged stock. It might be thought that the time lag between a change in the money supply and the response of the economy would be shorter than usual if the explanation for the change in monetary growth is an expenditure item and longer than usual if it is financial. The author undertook various studies in the 1970s to ascertain whether this was so. The general conclusion was that it was not, but the private sector's purpose in borrowing from banks may be important.

11.4.8 Reasons for Borrowing from a Bank

There was a boom in the provision of bank credit in the early 1970s and another one in the mid-1980s. On the first occasion the bulk of the initial lending was to finance expenditure on goods and services whereas on the latter it was to acquire financial assets. This is one of the reasons why the early outcome on the first occasion was product-price inflation whereas it was asset-price inflation on the second.

Elaborating, in the 1970s the government borrowed from banks to finance subsidies and price restraint by public corporations. There was also a prices and wages policy that restricted increases in prices more than wages. This reduced the cash flow of companies and industry had to borrow more from banks as a result. The bank deposits created by this borrowing entered people's income stream and subsequently tended to be spent on goods and services, the prices of which then rose.

In the 1980s much of the initial borrowing from banks was to finance the acquisition of assets. The bank deposits which this created were received by sellers of the assets and these tended to be savings deposits.

Asset prices rose when these were reinvested. Subsequently the increase in wealth and boost to financial confidence encouraged people to increase their spending on goods and services. The eventual effect was product-price inflation but it took longer to appear than it did in the 1970s. It was an explanation for an unusually long time lag in the 1980s.

APPENDIX 11.1   TWO TYPES OF MONETARY DISEQUILIBRIUM

Some people argue that the supply of money cannot be out of balance with the demand for it in other than the very short term. They reason that the money market is efficient in the sense that rates of interest alter to bring supply and demand quickly into line; that is, in technical language, that the market clears.

At first sight this seems correct. Most banks tend to manage their liabilities rather than their assets; they bid for whatever funds are needed to finance their holdings of assets rather than purchasing or selling assets in accordance with what is happening to their deposits. A bank short of funds bids higher rates in the money market. A bank flush with funds turns money away by offering unattractive rates. In other words banks adjust relative interest rates until they attract the desired amount of deposits. It might be thought that such action would bring the demand for money into line with supply.

A practical example shows that this is not so. Suppose that the starting point is a position of equilibrium with the demand and supply of money equal. Suppose that an industrialist decides to take over another company, payment being made in cash, and that the take-over is financed by borrowing from banks. When the take-over goes through the investors who held the ordinary shares of the company will receive the cash; that is, their bank deposits will increase. This will match banks' need for funds to finance the increase in their loans to the industrialist. Banks will not be short of finance and will not have to bid for additional funds. (This appendix ignores banks' need for additional liquid assets, etc.) Investors' portfolios will however have altered. Holdings of ordinary shares will be lower and bank deposits will be higher. Many investors will be dissatisfied with the increase in their bank deposits and will wish to reinvest the money in other ordinary shares. (There may be a general rise in the market because of the take-over but this will not discourage many investors from acting in due course to restore their portfolios to balance.) From banks' point of view the supply of bank deposits from their customers will be in line with what they, the banks, need. In this sense supply and demand will be equal, but as far as banks' customers are concerned the level of bank deposits will exceed demand.

Another example is someone borrowing from a bank to finance expenditure on goods and services. In this case the deposit created by the loan will be received by the provider of the goods and services. It will most likely be part of an income stream to be spent in due course on other goods and services. Such deposits remain in the banking system without banks having to bid for them. As far as banks are concerned their need for deposits will be in line with supply. As far as their customers are concerned the increase in bank deposits may be unintended saving that in due course will be spent on goods and services, leading to an acceleration in economic activity. Again the situation will not be one of equilibrium in the economy as a whole.

A rather different example is a government printing money. In this case the government borrows from the banking system and the increase in banks' holdings of government debt is matched by the growth in deposits. There is no need for banks to bid for funds but the economy as a whole will not be in equilibrium.

The above examples indicate that a distinction must be made between what is happening to banks and what is happening in the economy as a whole. For the latter the demand for money can differ from supply and the imbalance can last many months.

Although it is not relevant to the main argument it appears from the above examples that banks always receive exactly the amount of deposits they need to finance an increase in their assets. Banks can nevertheless be 'short of money'.

Shortages are liable to occur on days on which the government has a surplus.[1] On such a day money flows out of the banking system into the Exchequer. The Bank of England then relieves the shortage by purchasing bills in the money market. If too few bills are purchased to relieve the shortage then banks' deposits with the Bank will fall below the level that banks desire. Money is then said to be short and rates of interest will rise as banks bid for funds to replenish these deposits. Conversely money is said to be easy if the Bank provides too much assistance. Money market shortages and surpluses depend on action by the central bank. Disequilibria for banks are distinct from monetary disequilibria in the economy as a whole.[2]

Summarising, a distinction must be made between what is happening to banks and what is happening outside the banking system. In the economy as a whole the demand for money can differ from supply and the imbalance can last many months.

12 The Forecasts of Other Monetarists

It was argued at the end of Chapter 4 that a strong test of the validity of monetarism was whether forecasts based on monetary analysis had a better record than forecasts using other methods. In Chapter 9 only the Greenwell predictions and the letters from the Liverpool Six were advanced as evidence. It might be thought that other monetarist predictions would also have been cited, in particular those of individual members of the Liverpool Six, especially the records of Tim Congdon, Patrick Minford and Alan Walters. The review of this other evidence has been deferred until this chapter so that Congdon's and Minford's different approaches could be discussed first.

As stated in Chapter 10, Minford believes that the focus should be on narrow money whereas Congdon believes that narrow money has no significance and concentrates entirely on broad money. The different natures of broad and narrow money were discussed in Chapter 11 and it should be appreciated that the author sides much more with Congdon than Minford. The author's understanding of the basic way in which the monetary system works is almost identical to Congdon's. The only significant difference, about which the author is aware (if monetary base control is ignored, see Section 3.4, p. 23), is that the author has found the behaviour of narrow money very helpful on certain crucial occasions. Narrow money must not be used in isolation but it can warn when the notoriously variable time-lag between a change in broad money and the response of the economy is likely to be unusual. In the author's opinion Congdon is merely unwise to disregard the behaviour of narrow money, because something useful can on occasions be learnt from it, but Minford's error is more basic. The UK monetary system does not conform in practice to some of the non-monetary theories that he stresses. Firstly, expectations are not as important as the theory of rational expectations suggests. Although with the benefit of hindsight it may appear that the prospects for the future should have been clear, at the time the outlook often seems to be highly uncertain and expectations are not strongly held. Secondly, markets are also not necessarily 'efficient' in the sense that supply and demand may not come quickly into balance as a result of price changes; that is, markets may not clear quickly. If supply and demand did come quickly into balance Congdon and the author would be wrong to argue that an excess or an inadequate supply of money is one of the basic forces driving the economy. It is not denied that these non-monetary theories add to knowledge and understanding of the economy but too much emphasis should not be placed on them. Minford's patchy forecasting record, described below, is, in the author's opinion, explained by too much stress being placed on the supplementary theories.

12.1   PATRICK MINFORD

Patrick Minford has a high profile as a forecaster. His forecasts were included in those examined by Burrell and Hall mentioned in Chapter 6 and he is one of the Chancellor's 'wise men' (see Note 1 of Chapter 10, p. 201). His formal forecasts are published in the University of Liverpool's *Quarterly Economic Bulletin*. They started in March 1980. The complete record of the forecasts of the growth of GDP and inflation is given in Tables 12.3 and 12.4 in Appendix 12.1.

12.1.1   Recessions

1979–81

Liverpool's formal forecasts did not start in time to predict the 1979–81 recession in advance of the event. Its first two forecasts were made in March and November 1980, which were after the start of the recession. These forecasts were less accurate than those of NIESR and LBS made at about the same time. In its March forecast Liverpool predicted that GDP would be unchanged in 1980 whereas LBS and NIESR predicted falls of 1.7 per cent and 0.5 per cent, respectively. In its November forecast Liverpool predicted that GDP would grow by 1.4 per cent in 1981, compared with LBS's prediction, made in October, of a fall of 0.6 per cent and NIESR's, made in November, that the fall would be 0.8 per cent. Liverpool's forecasts were therefore the worst of the three (but its forecasts of inflation were the best).

1990–2

Liverpool's most optimistic forecast of economic growth in 1990 (4.2 per cent) was made in March 1989. This forecast was then revised steadily downward to 1.5 per cent in March 1990. The clear warning that the slowdown would be more than temporary came in June 1990 when the forecast for 1991 was revised from 3.0 per cent to 1.9 per cent, as shown in Chart 12.1. The subsequent forecasts for 1991 were revised rapidly downward. The first one predicting a fall in GDP (−1.8 per cent) was published in March 1991, that is, a month after the first of the Liverpool Six's letters to *The Times*. Table 12.1 compares Liverpool's forecasts to those of NIESR and LBS. It will be seen that, even allowing for the fact that Liverpool's forecasts were made slightly later than those for NIESR and LBS, Liverpool was marginally the best.

Chart 12.1   Liverpool – growth of GDP: predictions for 1990 and 1991

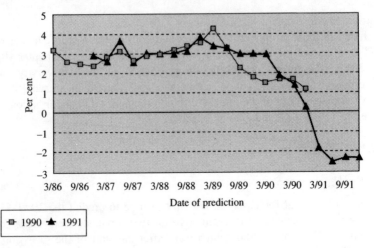

Table 12.1   Liverpool forecasts of growth of GDP in 1991

Liverpool		NIESR		LBS	
Date of forecast	*Forecast*	*Date of forecast*	*Forecast*	*Date of forecast*	*Forecast*
June 1990	1.9%	May 1990	2.7%	June 1990	2.1%
Sept 1990	1.5%	Aug 1990	1.9%		
Dec 1990	0.3%	Nov 1990	0.8%	Oct 1990	1.4%
March 1991	−1.8%	Feb 1991	−1.4%	Feb 1991	−0.8%
June 1991	−2.5%	May 1991	−2.2%	June 1991	−1.9%

12.1.2   Inflations

1989–90

In December 1987 Liverpool was forecasting that inflation in 1990 would be as low as 1.1 per cent but it then started to edge its forecast for that year upward, as shown in Chart 12.2. The first forecast for 1989 to be revised upward did not come until October 1988 when the prediction of inflation was raised from 1.4 per cent to 2.8 per cent; the prediction for 1990 was also increased at the same time, from 1.4 per cent to 2.2 per cent. Both predictions were far too low. Even as late as March 1989 Liverpool was forecasting that inflation in 1990 would be only 2.3 per cent. A month earlier LBS and NIESR had predicted 3.7 per cent and 5.9 per cent, respectively. Liverpool's forecast was clearly the worst of the three, the eventual outturn being 8 per cent.

Chart 12.2   Liverpool – inflation: predictions for 1989 and 1990

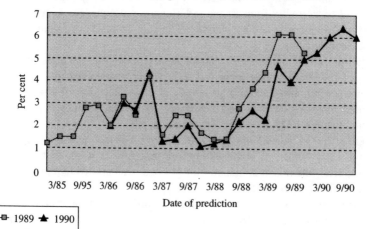

12.1.3   Summary

Judged by the criteria used in earlier chapters Liverpool's forecasting record has been patchy at best. Minford has nevertheless been mentioned many times in this book. His early work modelling rational expectations and the supply-side of the economy was acknowledged in Chapter 5. The author also paid tribute to him for valuable discussion that added much to the conclusions contained in the last chapter. Minford has a great deal to offer in terms of theory and analysis. Some of his insights are unique but a reliable forecasting record has not been one of his strengths.

12.2   ALAN WALTERS

Recapitulating on Chapter 1, Alan Walters wrote the *Sebag Gilt Edged Review* in the early 1970s; emigrated to the US in 1975; was the Prime Minister's personal economic adviser, either full-time or part-time, between 1980 and 1989, after which he returned to Washington.

Unfortunately the public record of Walters' forecasts is sparse. Copies of *Sebag Gilt Edged Review* do not appear to have survived and his forecasts were confidential while he was adviser to the Prime Minister. The main source of his views is his two books about the Thatcher years, that is, *Britain's Economic Renaissance, Margaret Thatcher's Reforms 1979–1984* (Walters: 1986) and *Sterling in Danger* (Walters: 1990).

In *Britain's Economic Renaissance* Walters asserts on page 118 that in 1971–2 he correctly forecast the inflationary consequences of the Barber boom. This is confirmed by Margaret Thatcher on p. 221 of *Path to Power* (see Section 1.3, p. 4).

On p. 145 of *Britain's Economic Renaissance* Walters states that he judged monetary policy to be too tight when he returned to London in January 1981 and had said so earlier at a seminar and briefing in the United States in October and November 1980. This implies that he predicted that the 1979–81 recession would deepen.

On p. 100 of *Sterling in Danger* Walters implies that he was not arguing in the early 1980s, as some unthinking monetarists were, that inflation would rise: 'the misleading nature of M3 had been argued by me from the end of 1980 and thereafter.'

On p. 94 of his second book Walters implies that in the mid-1980s he was forecasting that there would be steady non-inflationary growth of GDP: 'In my view the policy over the period 1983–6 was about as close as one could get to ideal.'

On pp. 102–3 Walters indicates that he started to become concerned about inflation as 1987 progressed and became alarmed in 1988:

From 1983 to mid-1986 the trend rate of growth of M0 was gently declining and, had it continued to decline at that rate, the goal of zero inflation would have been reached in 1990. The actual record, however, shows a marked increase of some 2 percentage points in the second half of 1986 ... As early as 1986 the writing was, albeit faintly, on the wall

... At least as far as M0 is concerned ... the change was initially small, almost imperceptible ... the divergence between a target path of zero inflation by 1990 and the actual growth rate of M0 expanded inexorably throughout 1987 and 1988. Finally, in September 1988, the growth rate of M0 rose to over 8 per cent and its divergence from the zero-inflation path grew to as much as 7 percentage points.

Some people may argue that the above extracts from *Sterling in Danger* are uncorroborated, but the author can confirm that they are correct. He was in close contact with Walters throughout the period and their views nearly always coincided.[1]

Finally Walters's forecast of the 1990–2 recession is on record as he was one of the Liverpool Six.

12.3   TIM CONGDON

Tim Congdon, like Patrick Minford, has a high profile as a forecaster and is another of the Chancellor's wise men. He joined the economics staff of *The Times* in 1973, having been recruited by Peter Jay. In 1976 he moved to the stockbrokers L. Messel & Co. but continued to write for the financial press, particularly for *The Times*. Messel was taken over by Shearson Lehman in 1987 and Congdon became their Chief London Economist for a short time before leaving to found Lombard Street Research in 1989 under the auspices of the discount house Gerrard & National.

12.3.1   1989–90 Inflation – Warnings Prior to October 1986

Prior to October 1986 Congdon, like the author, did not publish any formal economic forecasts and so an assessment of his early record is not straightforward. His main publication *Financial Analysis* started in 1979 and was circulated quarterly by Messel but this concentrated on forecasts of flow of funds (see Section 11.4.6, p. 171). He also wrote *Messel's Weekly Gilt Monitor* which from time to time contained predictions of the real economy and inflation, as did his newspaper and other articles. The most relevant ones are reproduced in his book *Reflections on Monetarism* (Congdon, 1992a) which is the best source of the forecasts he made prior to October 1986.

There is no doubt that Congdon was one of the very few economists to predict the inflationary consequences of the Lawson boom in time for remedial action to be taken. One criticism that is often heard needs answering. It is that his inflationary warnings were sounded much too soon. The first point to make in reply is that he was not one of those who erroneously forecast a rise in inflation following rapid growth of broad money in 1980, as the following quotation shows:

> The increase in sterling M3 in the three months to November [1980], a period relatively free from post-corset adjustment, was at an annual rate of nearly 20%. Against this background, is it reasonable to expect inflation to continue falling? Isn't the credibility of the government's whole macro-economic strategy in doubt? The difficulty with this bearish argument is that even the most doctrinaire monetarists regard a revival in economic activity as a necessary link in the causal chain between money and inflation. There is at present no convincing evidence of such a revival. (*Messel's Weekly Gilt Monitor*, 2 January 1981)

This quotation shows that Congdon not only allowed for obvious distortions to broad money, as discussed in Chapter 11, but also used judgement. A reading of the *Monitor* shows that he continued to argue throughout 1981 that there was no need for a rise in interest rates and that inflation would continue to fall.

The growth of broad money slowed in 1982 and any cause for concern from excessive monetary growth disappeared for a time. Monetary growth picked up again in 1985 and Congdon became worried as the year progressed. Even so he gave Nigel Lawson the benefit of the doubt right up to October 1985, as the following quotation shows:

> Despite all the unfavourable arithmetic [about the behaviour of the money supply], it would be unfair and wrong to start talking about the 'Lawson boom' ... There is a chance that the latest burst of high money growth will not be damaging in the long run. The economy has a reasonable margin of spare capacity and, with unemployment so high, there are no shortages of labour. If all goes well the latest phase of above-target money growth may lead solely to more output and not at all to higher prices. (*The Times*, 17 October 1985)

Congdon's serious warnings that inflation would rise started in January 1986, much later than some of his critics suggest.

12.3.2   Forecasts After October 1986

In 1986 Congdon recruited Peter Warburton from LBS and together they developed a large-scale macroeconomic model of the economy. The forecasts emanating from this model started in October 1986 but the record is a short one as Congdon left Shearson soon after, his last forecast being dated May/June 1988. Congdon claims that the forecasts before he resigned from Shearson were the most accurate ones of the British economy for both 1987 and 1988. For example he won the 'Golden Guru' award in 1988. (The 'Golden Guru' awards were made by Mr Christopher Hume of *The Independent on Sunday*.) In particular it must be noted that Congdon was consistent with his predictions of the inflation that would follow the Lawson boom; he did not wobble after the 1987 stock-market crash as did the author. As stated earlier, there is no doubt that Congdon was one of the very few economists to predict the inflationary consequences of the Lawson boom in time for remedial action to be taken. He should be given great credit for this.

Following his departure from Shearson Congdon's next formal forecast was made in December 1989 after he had established Lombard Street Research. For reference, Tables 12.5 and 12.6 in Appendix 12.1 give Lombard Street's forecasts of growth of GDP and inflation since they started.

12.3.3   Warning of the 1990–2 Recession

Lombard Street Research's forecasts only started just before the 1990–2 and so there is no record of any early warning about 1990. Table 12.2 shows the sequence of forecasts for the growth of GDP in 1991. It is an extension of Table 12.1, which compared Liverpool's forecasts with those of LBS and NIESR. It will be seen that Lombard Street's forecasts made in the second half of 1990 were not particularly good. In July 1990 the forecast was that the rate of growth of GDP in 1991 would be 2.1 per cent which was faster than the 1.9 per cent predicted by NIESR a month later. Lombard Street's October forecast (1.2 per cent) was however slightly more accurate than that of LBS. Once 1991 had started Lombard Street's performance improved and its record was the best of the four forecasting bodies if allowance is made for the month in which a forecast was made. In January for example Lombard Street was first of the forecasters to predict a fall in GDP (−1.5 per cent).

Table 12.2 Lombard Street Research forecasts of growth of GDP in 1991

Lombard Street		Liverpool		NIESR		LBS	
Date of forecast	Forecast	Date of forecast	Forecast	Date of forecast	Forecast	Date of forecast	Forecast
March 1990	2.4%	June 1990	1.9%	May 1990	2.7%	June 1990	2.1%
July 1990	2.1%	Sept 1990	1.5%	Aug 1990	1.9%		
Oct 1990	1.2%	Dec 1990	0.3%	Nov 1990	0.8%	Oct 1990	1.4%
Jan 1991	-1.5%	March 1991	-1.8%	Feb 1991	-1.4%	Feb 1991	-0.8%
Apr 1991	-2.4%	June 1991	-2.5%	May 1991	-2.2%	June 1991	-1.9%

12.4 OVERALL CONCLUSION

The conclusion is that Congdon's forecasting record of the 1989–90 inflation and the 1990–2 recession is a very creditable one. The record is however only over a short period of time. The author argues that it should be treated as an extension of his own forecasting record, as his and Congdon's basic insights into the workings of the monetary system are almost identical. The two records together cover a sufficiently long span of time to be evidence of the validity of monetarism.

There is a further point. As time has passed the analysis has been developed and improved. Chapter 11 illustrated how the author's thinking has clarified. Particular attention should be drawn to Congdon's more recent work on sectoral flow of funds, the behaviour of the corporate and personal sectors, the way in which they interact and the effects on the price of houses and personal wealth (see his various article in Gerrard & National's *Monthly Economic Review*). The evidence submitted in this book about the accuracy of monetarist forecasts of the economy is in accordance with the state of knowledge at the time the forecasts were made. As additional knowledge is gained the forecasting record should improve.

184

APPENDIX 12.1 REFERENCE TABLES

Table 12.3 Liverpool forecasts of growth of GDP

Year	3/80[a]	11/80[a]	3/81[a]	6/81[a]	10/81[a]	2/82[a]	6/82[a]	11/82	12/82	2/83	5/83	9/83	12/83	3/84	5/84	10/84	12/84	3/85	6/85	9/85	12/85	3/86	6/86	9/86	12/86
1980	0.0	1.9																							
1981	1.6	1.4	−0.2	−0.5	−1.3																				
1982	2.9	3.3	2.9	3.2	2.5	2.5	2.5	1.5	1.3																
1983	2.7	2.7	2.8	2.8	4.5	4.4	4.7	3.0	2.9	3.3	3.0	3.6	3.6												
1984	2.5	2.5	2.7	2.9	4.2	4.4	4.5	3.2	3.0	5.1	4.8	3.7	3.7												
1985							2.6	3.1	3.5	2.3	2.7	4.3	4.3	3.5	3.6	2.3	2.4	3.5	3.0	3.4	3.4	3.4	3.5	2.7	2.6
1986								3.5		3.8	3.9	4.1	4.4	3.0	3.0	3.2	4.4	3.8	4.0	3.0	3.0	3.6	3.1	3.1	3.0
1987														4.3	3.5	4.1	3.4	3.6	3.6	3.4	3.5	3.8	3.5	3.4	2.9
1988														4.0	3.1	2.7	2.8	3.4	2.9	3.4	3.3	3.9	2.6	3.6	2.8
1989																2.4	4.2	2.9	3.2	3.2	3.3	3.8	2.6	2.5	2.4
1990																	3.5					3.2			2.9
1991																									
1992																									
1993																									
1994																									
1995																									

Table 12.3   (Continued)

Year	3/87	6/87	10/87	12/87	3/88	6/88	10/88	12/88	3/89	6/89	10/89	12/89	3/90	6/90	10/90	12/90	3/91	6/91	10/91	12/91	3/92	6/92	10/92	12/92	3/93
1980																									
1981																									
1982																									
1983																									
1984																									
1985																									
1986																									
1987	3.3	2.9	3.1	3.4																					
1988	3.3	2.9	3.0	2.5	3.0	3.0	3.8	3.8																	
1989	3.8	2.7	2.6	2.6	2.8	3.3	3.0	3.6	3.4	2.8	1.7	1.9													
1990	2.8	3.1	2.7	2.9	3.0	3.2	3.4	3.6	4.3	3.3	2.3	1.8	1.5	1.7	1.7	1.2	-1.8	-2.5	-2.3	-2.3					
1991	2.6	3.6	2.6	3.0	3.0	3.0	3.2	3.8	3.4	3.3	3.0	3.0	3.0	1.9	1.5	0.3	0.7	0.4	0.3	0.3	-0.1	-0.5	-0.9	-0.9	
1992				3.2	2.7	2.9	3.4	3.3	3.4	3.4	3.1	3.2	3.5	2.9	2.9	2.6	1.7	2.6	2.5	3.3	1.9	1.2	2.0	0.1	0.3
1993												4.0	3.9	2.8	3.1	3.1	3.1	3.5	3.4	3.8	3.8	2.3	3.2	2.9	2.6
1994													4.0	3.6	3.7	3.0	3.0	3.6	3.2	2.7	3.5	2.8	2.7	3.6	3.4
1995																									

Table 12.3   (Continued)

Year	6/93	10/93	12/93	3/94	6/94	10/94	12/94
1980							
1981							
1982							
1983							
1984							
1985							
1986							
1987							
1988							
1989							
1990							
1991							
1992							
1993	0.7	1.7	1.8	3.0	2.9	3.4	3.8
1994	2.1	3.2	3.3	3.1	3.1	3.4	3.5
1995	3.1	3.2	3.0				

Notes:
Percentage growth of GDP at factor cost, expenditure estimate except where indicated.
[a] Average estimate.

Source: *Quarterly Economic Report*, Liverpool University, Dec. 1987 and Oct. 1990 updated.

Table 12.4 Liverpool forecasts of inflation

Year	3/80	11/80	3/81	6/81	10/81	2/82	6/82	11/82	12/82	2/83	5/83	9/83	12/83	3/84	5/84	10/84	12/84	3/85	6/85	9/85	12/85	3/86	6/86	9/86	12/86
1980	16.5	18.0																							
1981	9.0	8.1	9.5	11.1	11.3																				
1982	8.1	5.0	5.4	6.4	7.6	7.6	7.6	7.7	7.7																
1983	4.3	4.1	4.2	4.4	4.2	4.0	4.3	4.0	4.0	4.4	4.5	4.6	4.6												
1984	1.4	2.9	3.5	4.2	5.2	4.1	4.4	4.5	4.1	1.5	1.8	2.2	3.3	3.4	3.7	4.5	4.5								
1985							4.1	5.8	5.2	1.5	1.9	1.6	1.2	2.1	2.1	2.3	3.1	3.7	3.8	4.3	4.8	3.2	3.8	3.7	3.8
1986										2.4	0.9	1.9	0.7	0.9	1.4	2.0	2.2	2.7	2.6	3.6	3.3	2.4	2.8	3.4	3.6
1987													0.7	0.5	1.3	0.6	2.1	1.8	1.8	2.7	2.5	2.0	2.5	2.4	3.6
1988																0.0	1.3	1.9	1.9	3.0	2.7	2.0	3.3	2.5	3.6
1989																	1.2	1.5	1.5	2.8	2.9	2.0	3.0	2.7	4.2
1990																									4.3
1991																									4.0
1992																									
1993																									
1994																									
1995																									

Table 12.4 (Continued)

Year	3/87	6/87	10/87	12/87	3/88	6/88	10/88	12/88	3/89	6/89	10/89	12/89	3/90	6/90	10/90	12/90	3/91	6/91	10/91	12/91	3/92	6/92	10/92	12/92	3/93
1980																									
1981																									
1982																									
1983																									
1984																									
1985																									
1986																									
1987	3.3	3.7	3.7	3.3																					
1988	1.9	2.7	3.1	2.4	2.8	2.6	3.6	4.2																	
1989	1.6	2.5	2.5	1.7	1.4	1.4	2.8	3.7	4.4	6.1	6.1	5.3													
1990	1.3	1.4	2.0	1.1	1.2	1.4	2.2	2.7	2.3	4.7	4.0	5.0	5.3	6.0	6.4	6.0									
1991	1.3	1.7	1.4	0.7	1.0	1.6	1.3	1.8	2.5	3.0	3.3	4.6	4.4	5.3	5.4	5.7	5.8	6.1	6.1	6.5					
1992				0.9	1.5	1.4	1.2	2.2	0.9	1.5	3.3	3.5	3.4	4.2	4.2	3.3	3.7	4.6	4.2	4.0	3.2	3.7	5.1	5.2	
1993												2.2	2.5	3.6	3.3	2.3	4.8	4.6	4.4	4.4	3.9	3.8	5.7	3.1	3.9
1994													2.0	2.4	2.2	2.1	4.7	3.8	3.9	3.9	3.8	3.0	4.2	3.3	2.8
1995																	3.6	3.6	4.1	4.9	3.2	1.9	3.4	2.7	3.3

Table 12.4 (Continued)

Year	6/93	10/93	12/93	3/94	6/94	10/94	12/94
1980							
1981							
1982							
1983							
1984							
1985							
1986							
1987							
1988							
1989							
1990							
1991							
1992							
1993	3.8	2.9	3.4				
1994	3.3	2.2	2.0	2.0	2.8	2.5	
1995	3.7	2.5	2.8	1.8	2.2	2.0	

Note:

Percentage change in consumer price index, calendar year comparisons.

Source: Quarterly Economic Bulletin, Liverpool University, Dec. 1987 and Oct. 1990 updated.

Table 12.5   Lombard Street Research forecasts of growth of GDP (percentage growth)

Year being forecast	Date of forecast																								
	12/89	3/90	7/90	10/90	1/91	4/91	7/91	10/91	1/92	4/92	7/92	10/92	2/93	4/93	7/93	10/93	2/94	4/94	7/94	10/94	2/95	4/95	7/95	10/95	1/96
1989	2.6	2.1	2.1																						
1990	0.4	0.5	0.2	0.8	1.3	0.7	0.6																		
1991	2.1	2.4	2.1	1.2	−1.5	−2.4	−2.4	−2.3	−2.4	−2.4	−2.4														
1992					2.1	1.9	2.0	2.0	0.6	0.2	−0.8	−1.1	−0.9	−0.5	−0.5										
1993									2.8	2.1	0.8	1.3	1.1	1.5	1.6	1.8	2.0	1.9	1.9						
1994													3.4	2.9	2.9	2.5	3.0	3.4	3.4	3.6	4.0	3.9	3.9		
1995																	3.5	3.5	3.3	2.7	2.7	2.5	2.7	2.8	2.6

Note:
Expenditure estimate prior to April 1992, average estimate thereafter.

Table 12.6   Lombard Street Research forecasts of inflation (percentage change in retail price index)

Year being forecast	Date of forecast																								
	12/89	3/90	7/90	10/90	1/91	4/91	7/91	10/91	1/92	4/92	7/92	10/92	2/93	4/93	7/93	10/93	2/94	4/94	7/94	10/94	2/95	4/95	7/95	10/95	1/96
1989	8.1	7.7																							
1990	7.4	7.0	8.8	9.4	10.0																				
1991	7.0	5.2	4.8	4.6	5.2	4.0	4.0	4.5	4.2																
1992					4.0	2.0	2.0	2.0	2.8	2.8	3.1	3.2	3.1												
1993									1.5	1.3	1.4	2.6	2.1	1.5	1.7	1.9	1.6								
1994													1.0	1.0	1.9	1.5	1.8	1.9	2.2	2.6	2.6				
1995																	2.0	2.6	2.6	2.3	2.7	2.8	2.8	3.2	3.2

13 Conclusions and Policy Implications

13.1 FINE-TUNING THE ECONOMY

- Forecasts of the economy are inaccurate; the average margin of error is 1 per cent of GDP or more. This is true whether the forecasts are Keynesian or monetarist and whether or not use is made of a macro-economic model of the economy.
- Because of the inaccuracy, attempts should not be made to predict minor fluctuations in the business cycle.
- Because the state of knowledge is inadequate to be able to do so successfully, attempts should not be made to fine-tune the economy.

13.2 MAJOR ECONOMIC EVENTS

- Forecasters should focus their attention on trying to predict major events that are, or should be, within the margin of accuracy of their techniques.
- In the 1970s and 1980s the macroeconomic models did not predict major economic events in time for action to be taken to avoid the event; they did little better than report an event as it started to occur.
- The current approach to economic management, which relies largely on judgement, was ineffective in the 1970s and 1980s; it did not prevent either the Barber or the Lawson boom.
- As it is not possible to fine-tune the economy, the economy's self-stabilisers should be improved as much as possible.
- An example of a self-stabiliser is the automatic rise in the public sector borrowing requirement (PSBR) that occurs in a recession (because of lost revenue and higher unemployment benefits, etc.) and the automatic fall in a boom. Providing that the average PSBR over the business cycle is not excessive such automatic changes should be allowed to materialise.

13.3 MONEY SUPPLY POLICY

- The policy of announcing targets for the money supply with the aim of influencing expectations and for political purposes was a failure in the 1980s; reliance should not be placed on such a policy in the future.
- Monetary analysis in the 1970s and 1980s was reasonably efficient at predicting major events providing allowance was made for distortions to the aggregates but the precise timing of an event was not forecast.
- The warnings were given in time for remedial action to be taken.
- The worst of the Barber and Lawson booms would have been avoided if the warnings from monetary analysis had been heeded.
- There were occasions when the monetary barometers were jammed; this should have been known at the time and the barometers should have been declared temporarily out of order.

13.4 CONTROL OF THE MONEY SUPPLY

There are various degrees in which the money supply can be used either as an indicator or as a factor to be controlled, for example:

- Discretionary measures can be based on warnings from monetary analysis. The danger of such a policy is that too little action may be taken too late, as in the past, in which case more powerful measures will be needed later on and the disruption to the economy will be worse.
- Direct action can be taken to rectify obviously excessive or inadequate monetary growth. This brings forward remedial action, in which case measures should not need to be so powerful and the disruption to the economy should be less. Providing allowance is made for distortions, this type of monetary control will act as a powerful self-stabiliser for the economy.

13.5 HOW QUICKLY SHOULD THE AUTHORITIES REACT TO UNDESIRABLE MONETARY GROWTH?

- The shorter is the reaction time, the greater is the chance that action turns out to be unnecessary and of needless disruption to the economy.
- Fluctuations in the money supply that last for less than six months should definitely be ignored.

- Assuming that the warning from the monetary aggregates is not a false alarm, the longer is the reaction time the more powerful need be the measures and the greater the consequential disruption to the economy.
- A balance needs to be struck between disruption from unnecessary measures and increased disruption because necessary measures have been delayed.

13.6   THE OPTIMUM SOLUTION[1]

- The optimum solution is to leave the reaction time to discretion. Judgement should be based on how clear the situation is at the time.
- If the situation is clear, for example if the monetary aggregates are all behaving in a similar way, the reaction time might be as short as six months.
- If most of the aggregates are distorted but the message from them can nevertheless be discerned with a reasonable degree of confidence after analysis, the reaction time might be about a year.
- If the aggregates are all distorted, because for example of financial innovation, policy should be based on an overall judgement of the economic situation and not on the behaviour of the monetary aggregates until the message from the aggregates becomes clearer.

Notes

Introduction and Summary

1   The Centre for Economic Forecasting at LBS was founded by Jim Ball (now Sir James) and Terry Burns (now Sir Terence). The latter became director of the Centre in 1976. He was determined to make correct forecasts and investigated any that were better than his own. Monetarism soon came to his notice. He used to return to his office in the evening and play with the LBS model. In the morning his colleagues would not know what they would find. The author suspected that Burns had a simple monetary model in his mind, that he used it to predict the behaviour of GDP in money terms, and that he then tuned the main model to give the same answer and to fill in the details, paying particular attention to the international transmission mechanism of monetary policy (as explained in Chapter 5). Whatever his method, the results were most successful. In 1980 Burns became Chief Economic Adviser to the Treasury at the age of only 35. His forecasting record continued at first to be excellent. The most brilliant forecast of which the author is aware was the one Burns made in a speech to the Economic Club of New York in November 1980 when he predicted that the recession would bottom in about the spring. He subsequently lost his touch as a forecaster because, in the author's opinion, he had stayed too long in the public sector. He in effect changed jobs in 1991 when he succeeded Peter Middleton as Permanent Secretary of the Treasury, that is, head of the Treasury. He was in turn succeeded by Alan Budd who had earlier succeeded him has Director of the Centre for Economic Forecasting at LBS.

PART I   HOW THE MONETARISTS CAME TO POWER

Chapter 1   Early Monetarism in the UK

1.   In 1959–60 there were no statistics of the quantity of money in the UK and Alan Walters applied for a Houblon Norman grant from the Bank of England to develop monetary statistics similar to those of the US. He was turned down on the grounds that the Radcliffe Committee had considered that the money stock was not important!
2.   The author was the editor of Greenwell's *Monetary Bulletin* until well into the 1980s. As 1982 progressed he found that, having been appointed joint senior partner of W. Greenwell & Co., there was less and less time available to originate a *Bulletin*; they were discussed with him but he was not the primary editor. In 1983 the frequent absence of his initials at the end of a

Bulletin signified that there had not even been time to discuss the contents
before circulation and the character of the *Bulletin* subsequently altered.
Some of the author's speeches were, however, circulated under the *Bulletin*
banner.

In the mid-1980s W. Greenwell & Co. was taken over by Samuel
Montagu & Co. as part of the upheaval in the UK securities industry (the
'Big Bang') and the firm became part of Midland Group. The author gave
up executive responsibility and started to write a second series of the
Bulletin in June 1987 (they were circulated under the name of Midland
Montagu, the investment banking and securities arm of the Group, to distin-
guish them from the *Gilt Edged Market Background* circulated by
Greenwell Montagu Gilt-Edged). The last in the second series was circu-
lated in October 1989.

3. The surveys were started by the Continental Illinois International
Corporation. These were published annually and remained the most authoritative until well into the 1980s.

4. Another of the original 'teenage scribblers' was Dr Paul Nield of Philips
and Drew, who was rated the best analyst of the economy.

Chapter 2   Greenwell's *Monetary Bulletin*

1. The author was influenced by and would like to pay tribute to Robert
Nield who was his supervisor during his last year at Trinity College.
Robert had had a spell in the Treasury and been the first editor of the
National Institute Quarterly Review. He subsequently joined the
Department of Economic Affairs under George Brown (the late Lord
George-Brown). Robert eventually returned to Cambridge and became a
close associate of Wynne Godley.

2. The author's postgraduate training in economics came in effect from Harold
Rose, to whom he would like to pay tribute. Harold was Greenwell's
economic adviser. He had founded the Prudential Assurance Co.'s economics
department, before going to LSE and then LBS; he was also the author of
Economic Background to Investment (Rose 1960) which at the time was the
standard text book on the subject. (Later on Harold was too busy to become
consultant to the *Bulletin*.)

3. Geoffrey Wood became Professor of Economics at City University Business
School alongside Brian Griffiths.

4. A little while after the start of the *Bulletin* we heard rumours that some
people thought that the explanation of how we managed to circulate them so
quickly was that the Bank was giving us advance information. The Bank
subsequently changed the time of release of data for the money supply to
2.30 p.m. We guessed most of the contents of the first edition of *Banking
Statistics* released at this time, wrote most of the *Bulletin* in advance and
delivered it to our clients by 4.15 p.m.!

5. The *Bulletin* was utilised later on. The Bank used to have biennial training
courses for its high flyers that were held at the London Business School.
Eddie George, when he was in charge of the gilt-edged market, asked the
author to give one of the lectures. The author asked George if he was sure,

as he would be critical of the Bank. George's reply was that he wanted the high flyers to hear both sides of arguments and to be made to think. The *Bulletin* in the safe was the basis for the lecture.

(Peter Middleton (see Chapter 4, note 2) had suggested in 1974 that the author should get to know Eddie George after the latter had returned to the Bank after a spell with the IMF (latterly as assistant to the chairman of the Group of Twenty). George was described as an official's official. He became Deputy Chief Cashier in 1977, Assistant Director (Gilt-edged Division) in 1980, which was when the author came to know him better, Executive Director in charge of domestic monetary policy in 1982, Deputy Governor in 1990 and finally Governor in 1993. As Governor George is remarkable because he is a market-man rather than a banker. His predecessors have been afraid of disorderly markets and this has interfered with the implementation of monetary policy. George is much more sanguine because of his better understanding of markets. This was illustrated at a meeting of the Society of Investment Analysts, now the Institute of Investment Management and Research, in the late 1970s. At the meeting George appeared to accept that the Bank had allowed 'the bears to get back in', as asserted in the *Bulletin* that was never circulated, but he went on to argue that the Bank had to do so because the PSBR was at the time extremely high. He stated that he would teach the bears a lesson as soon as he could. Many did not believe him but in due course he did exactly as he promised. This story is relevant because George is motivated by 'love of the Bank'; he will do his utmost to enhance the credibility of the Bank and monetary policy. He dearly wishes that it was the same as the Bundesbank. Some may argue that he will not dare to issue a public warning if he thinks that there is a serious danger that inflation will rise because of the effect it would have on the gilt-edged market and on sterling. They are wrong.)

6.   The perks were also better. According to rumour, when officials of the Bank and the Treasury were abroad the former stayed at a better hotel and the Bank footed the bill for dinner together!

7.   Later on mandatory deposits were lowered to one half per cent of eligible liabilities; they were extended to all banks; the financing of the Bank was made explicit; and any excess endowment element in its profits was passed by the Bank to the Treasury.

Chapter 3   Fly on the Wall during the Thatcher Revolution

1.   Charles Goodhart once promised the author that he would show him the précis of the *Bulletins* after sufficient time had elapsed but he never did.

2.   Peter Lilley subsequently became MP for St Albans, Nigel Lawson's PPS, Financial Secretary to the Treasury, Minister of State for Industry and, at the time of writing, Secretary of State for Social Security.

3.   See references to money managers, monetarist theories and 'teenage scribblers' in Healey (1989: 412–13, 434).

4.   The same does not apply to currency boards. Dominions and ex-colonies that have become independent tend to have central banks. Colonies that

are not independent, for example Hong Kong, tend to have currency boards.

5.   After the Conservatives had won the election in May 1979 the author was approached to see if he would be willing to do the same job for the leader of the Labour Party, Mr Callaghan (now Lord Callaghan), as he had for Mrs Thatcher. Under the UK's political system the party in opposition has no civil servants nor does it have a well-endowed major institution on which it can rely, such as the Brookings Institute in the US. The Civil Service advises the government and contact between it and the Opposition is through advisers and not direct. The result can be that the Opposition is not well briefed. The invitation was to a meeting with Mr Callaghan to see if he wanted the author to help brief him. It was declined.

6.   In the mid-1970s the author received a letter from Keynes's nephew saying that he had seen the Great Man shortly before he died and reporting that Keynes had realised what his followers were likely to do in his name and was very gloomy about it.

7.   Greenwell were at one time asked to give daily reports about what was happening in the gilt-edged market direct to the US Treasury. The Secretary of the Treasury at the time was Bill Simon, who had been a partner of Salomon Brothers, the US investment bank that then specialised in bonds. It appeared that a bond man wanted to hear from another what was really happening. We reported the request to the Bank who raised no objection. The author wonders if the Economic Minister at our Embassy in Washington knew about the reports.

8.   Wynne Godley was an advocate of a siege economy, although he will probably not agree with this description. He and the author did a duo at a meeting of Harvard and London Business School Alumni. The audience were surprised at the amount of agreement reached between two people who apparently represented totally opposite views. Godley and the author agreed on the serious situation confronting the UK. Much of the diagnosis was similar. The departure came with the proposed remedies.

9.   In the author's view believers in the theory of rational expectations did a disservice suggesting that the cure for inflation would be painless if the government convinced people that the policy would be followed.

10.   In fact the Conservative government came close to an even more dangerous policy in 1980. It was the intermediate one of sustained pressure significantly more severe than advocated by gradualists. The monetary pressure was neither restricted to a level deemed to be safe nor was it of strictly limited duration. It scared the author and *Bulletin* no. 106, June 1980 (see Section A.9.1.7, p. 146) warned of the danger that the result could be an enforced U-turn. The author learnt later that Mrs Thatcher had objected when she thought that he had used the expression U-turn in an earlier article in *The Observer* and he was dismissed from her thoughts with the remark 'I thought he was one of us.' In fact the words were not the author's. They were contained in the headline written by William Keegan which had not been seen in advance of publication.

Chapter 4   Monetarism in 1980s

1.   The detailed behaviour of the monetary aggregates in the 1980s is discussed in Pepper (1990b).
2.   According to rumour Peter Middleton (now Sir Peter) wrote the introduction to *Monetary Control*. Between 1969 and 1972 he was Private Secretary to the Chancellor of the Exchequer. He was appointed Treasury Press Secretary in 1972, after Anthony Barber started to obtain a bad press, and became the most outward-going press secretary that the Treasury has ever had, which was when the author got to know him. In 1975 Middleton was appointed head of the Treasury's Monetary Policy Division and the contact between him and the author became closer. Middleton too was very worried about the UK economy, accepted that 'we could not go on like this', and was searching for a way forward. He first met Margaret Thatcher when she was leader of the Opposition at a secret meeting at the author's home, which illustrates the lack of direct contact between officials and the Opposition. Middleton succeeded Sir Douglas Wass as Permanent Secretary of the Treasury in 1984. He resigned to enter the private sector in 1993.
3.   It may be noted that the chairman of one of the banks that grew very quickly used to be deputy governor of the Bank and, while in that position, argued against monetarism.
4.   In his review of *Money, Credit and Asset Prices* (Pepper 1994), Kent Matthews wrote: 'this to my mind is one of the best chapters in the book. It should be compulsory reading for all budding monetary economists trained in the methods of modern econometrics who appear to pay scant attention to the data they use' (Matthews 1995).
5.   In the original version of the paper the section on each distortion contained a paragraph reporting the first mention of it in a *Bulletin*.

PART II   THE VALIDITY OF MONETARISM: ECONOMIC FORECASTS IN THE 1970s AND 1980s

Chapter 5   A Brief History of Macroeconomic Models

1.   This account relies heavily on Ball and Holly (1991: 195–230).
2.   An example of an identity is that GDP is defined in the *National Income Accounts* to be (i) consumer expenditure, plus (ii) general government consumption, plus (iii) total fixed investment, plus (iv) exports of goods, plus (v) change in stocks, less (vi) imports of goods and services, less (vii) an adjustment to factor cost.
3.   The dates are for the provision of public finance; some of the activities continued after this financial support ceased.
4.   The LBS model was originally based on the Wharton model in the USA, in the tradition of Klein and Goldberger.

Chapter 6   The Accuracy of Routine Forecasts

1. As well as LBS, NIESR and HMT the academic group consisted of Cambridge Economics (formerly The Cambridge Economic Growth Project), City University Business School (since ceased, Michael Beenstock) and Liverpool University (Patrick Minford). The second group comprised the Confederation of British Industries, Henley Centre for Economic Forecasting and Oxford Economic Forecasting. The third was made up of James Capel, Goldman Sachs (Gavin Davies), Robert Fleming, Laing and Cruikshank, Lombard Street Research (Tim Congdon), Philips and Drew (Bill Martin) and Shearson Lehman.

Chapter 8   The Record of the Large Models

1. A table is included in NIESR's current *Quarterly Reviews* giving medium-term forecasts; these are intended to be taken 'as indicative of the general direction in which the economy is moving rather than a specific forecast of a particular variable for a particular time'.
2. Deeming the prediction to be wholly data is not being completely fair to the National Institute because there is a delay between preparing the forecast and the date of the publication. The forecast was in fact prepared before data for the December RPI were published in the middle of January.
3. Prior to LBS's *Economic Outlook* forecasts were published in the *Sunday Times*. The data given are from *Economic Outlook*.
4. In 1976 the *Autumn Statement* was released in December rather than November.
5. The forecasts made 38 months in advance are the earliest made by LBS; the first of these was for 1981 and was made when the forecasts started in October 1977.
6. NIESR's predictions 13 months in advance started with the one for 1980 which was made in November 1978. They stopped after the one for 1989 made in November 1987.

Chapter 9   A Monetarist Forecast

1. This *Bulletin* was memorable for the author because an ex-Chief Economic Adviser of the Treasury refused to discuss it because, according to him, it was 'schoolboy' economics and an ex-Deputy Chief Economic Adviser described it as not even A level Economics.
2. The author was *not* one of the 364 economists who wrote to *The Times* predicting depression after the tightening of fiscal policy in the March 1981 budget!
3. A warning about the danger of a speculative bubble being allowed to build up in the USA had been given by the author in June 1986 in a speech to the US Financial Analysts Federation:
    'The indications ... are that a financial bubble has not yet built up. So far, so good; but if I were a central bank governor watching the explosion of

credit I would pay close attention to the level of the common stock market to make sure that a bubble was not building up' (p. 3).

4.   Circulated by Greenwell Montagu Gilt-Edged.

5.   The date of writing the article.

6.   A post-mortem of the period is contained in Pepper (1990b):

Chancellor Lawson's first mistake was to think that M0 was a leading rather than a nearly coincidental indicator of money GDP. With a leading indicator, the authorities have time to take correct action but, if the indicator is merely coincidental, there is a danger that undesirable momentum builds up. His second mistake was to assume that he had an effective mechanism of control over M0 ... (p. 22)

... a rise in interest rates has very little direct impact on M0. The mechanism is the indirect one of an increase in interest rates affecting the economy in general and retail sales in particular. The slowdown in retail sales is then reflected in the behaviour of M0. This process can take some time to occur. Moreover, a rise in short-term interest rates may not have a powerful effect on the economy unless the rise is sufficiently large to constitute a definite shock ... (p. 23)

... the mechanism of control was adequate to correct only minor departures of M0 from its desired path. It was therefore essential that corrective action be taken promptly. Even so, it was most probably only a matter of time before a larger deviation occured, possibly because the authorities had earlier guessed the wrong level of interest rates. When this happened, interest rates would have had to be raised very aggressively.

Chancellor Lawson's third mistake was that he allowed himself to be diverted by the October 1987 crash in the stock markets. He was unlucky that retail sales, and hence M0, happened to fluctuate downward in a way which was consistent with the forecasts of recession at the time. His mistake of paying too much attention to the stock-market crash is very easy to understand. But his mechanism of control was not sufficiently robust to allow for bad luck.

Mr Lawson's fourth mistake came on top of the others. He allowed himself to be diverted into attempting to shadow the deutchmark in the spring of 1988. This was the crucial error. (p. 24)

PART III   REFINEMENTS, FURTHER EVIDENCE AND POLICY IMPLICATIONS

Chapter 10   The 'Liverpool Six'

1.   Norman Lamont succeeded John Major in November 1990 after the latter became Prime Minister. He publicly appointed seven 'wise men'. Tim Congdon and Patrick Minford were included. The others were Andrew Britton of NIESR, David Currie of LBS, Gavin Davies of Goldman Sachs, Wynne Godley from Cambridge and Andrew Sentance from the CBI. (He also appointed Bill Robinson as Special Adviser in 1991. Robinson had been a Senior Research Fellow at LBS from 1979 to 1986 when he left to become

director of the Institute of Fiscal Studies. Robinson resigned as Special Adviser when Norman Lamont was replaced by Kenneth Clarke in 1993.)
2.   Robert Miller was the editor of *Economic Affairs*.
3.   Graham Mather subsequently resigned as director of the IEA to found the European Policy Forum.

Chapter 11   The Current State of Knowledge

1.   Details are omitted here in the interest of simplicity. The relevant surplus is not only the public sector's financial position, as defined in the PSBR, but also settlement of transactions in public sector debt, for example, gilt-edged stock, and external transactions, for example changes in foreign exchange reserves.
2.   Confusion may also arise from the way banks acted in the early 1970s after a new regime of monetary control had been introduced (after the Bank had published its consultative document *Competition and Credit Control*). Under this banks were required to maintain a reserve asset ratio, the most important category of reserve assets being treasury bills. If there was a shortage of reserve assets the Bank thought that banks would sell some of their holdings of gilt-edged stock to finance purchases of treasury bills. In the event banks bid for additional funds by offering CDs at attractive rates, intending to use these funds to acquire treasury bills; that is, they managed their liabilities rather than their assets. The bidding for funds in the CD market gave the impression that banks were short of funds. Such bidding did in fact increase the amount of bank deposits. The explanation was that CD rates rose above treasury bill rates and this encouraged many non-bank holders of treasury bills to switch into CDs, the treasury bills being acquired by banks. The result was that government borrowing from non-banks was replaced by borrowing from banks and the money supply rose. The point is that the rise did not come about because banks were short of funds – banks' demand for funds did not exceed supply – but because they wanted to alter the composition of their assets to improve their reserve asset ratios.

Chapter 12   The Forecasts of Other Monetarists

1.   See Section 3.4, p. 24. More particularly, Walters paid attention to M0 whereas the author focused on non-interest-bearing M1 when assessing when to become concerned about excessive growth of broad money. Both of these narrow aggregates gave similar messages.

Chapter 13   Conclusions and Policy Implications

1.   Only demand-side control of the money supply is discussed. The author would in fact prefer supply-side control; that is, control of the monetary base, providing adequate buffers are included in the system of control. This subject is outside the scope of this book.

References

Ball, J. and Holly, S. (1991) 'Macroeconomic Model-Building in the United Kingdom', in Bodkin R. G., Klein L. R. and Marwals K. (eds) *A History of Macroeconomic Model-Building*, Edward Elgar, Aldershot, pp. 195–229.

Bank of England (various years) *Bank of England Quarterly Bulletin*, London.

Bank of England (various years) *Banking Statistics*, London.

Bank of England (1971) *Competition and Credit Control*, London.

Barker T. (1985) 'Forecasting the Economic Recession in the UK 1979–1982: A Comparison of Model-Based *ex ante* Forecasts', *Journal of Economic Forecasting*, vol. 4, pp. 133–51.

Benston, G. (1991) 'Does Regulation Produce Stability?', in Wood G. E. and Capie F. H. (eds), *Unregulated Banking: Chaos or Order*, Macmillan, London.

Britton, A. and Pain, N. (1992) *Economic Forecasting in Britain*, National Institute of Economic and Social Research, Report Series no. 4, London.

Burns, T. (1986) 'The Interpretation and Use of Economic Predictions', in J. Mason, P. Mathias and J. H. Wescott (eds) *Predictability in Science and Society*, Royal Society and British Academy, London, pp. 103–125.

Burrell, A. and Hall, S. (1993) 'A Comparison of Short-Term Macroeconomic Forecasts', London Business School.

Central Statistical Office (various years) *Financial Statistics*, London.

City University Business School (1981) *Annual Monetary Review*, London.

Clayton, G., Gilbert, J. C. and Sedgwick, R. (eds) (1971) *Monetary Theory and Monetary Policy*, Oxford University Press.

Congdon, T. (various years) *Financial Analysis*, L. Messel & Co., London.

Congdon, T. (various years) *Messel's Weekly Gilt Monitor*, L. Messel & Co., London.

Congdon, T. (various years) *Monthly Economic Review*, Gerrard & National, London.

Congdon, T. (1992a) *Reflections on Monetarism*, Edward Elgar/Institute of Economic Affairs, Aldershot.

Congdon, T. (1992b) 'Concept of Monetary Equilibrium: Its Significance for Narrow Money Versus Broad Money Debate', Money, Macro and Finance Research Group, ESRC, 1992, and *Monthly Economic Review*, Gerrard & National, no. 38, August, 1992.

Continental Illinois Corporation (various years) Annual Surveys of Investment Analysts, London.

Croome, D. and Johnson, H. G. (eds) (1970) *Money in Britain*, Oxford University Press.

Fforde, J. (1993) 'Setting Monetary Objectives', *Bank of England Quarterly Bulletin*, June, pp. 200–8.

Frenkel, J. A. and Johnson H. J. (eds) (1976) *The Monetary Approach to the Balance of Payments*, Allen & Unwin, London.

Friedman, M. (1960) *A Program for Monetary Stability*, Fordham University Press, New York.

Friedman, M. (1968) 'The Role of Monetary Policy', *American Economic Review*, 58, March, pp. 1–17.

Friedman, M. and Schwartz, A. (1963) *A Monetary History of the United States 1867–1960*, Princeton University Press, Princeton.

Greenwood, J. (various years in the late 1970s) *Asian Monetary Monitor*, GT Management, Hong Kong.

Griffiths, B. (various editions in the 1970s) *Pember & Boyle Review*, London.

Hayek, F. A. (1976) *The Road to Serfdom*, Routledge & Kegan Paul, London.

Healey, D. (1989) *The Time of My Life*, Michael Joseph, London.

Howe, G. (1994) *Conflict of Loyalty*, Macmillan, London.

Institute of Economic Affairs (various years) *Economic Affairs*, London.

Johnson, H. G. and Nobay, A. R. (eds) (1971) *The Current Inflation*, Macmillan, London.

Lawson, N. (1992) *The View from No. 11*, Bantam, London.

'Liverpool Six', namely Tim Congdon, Bill Martin, Patrick Minford, Gordon Pepper, Alan Walters and Peter Warburton (1991–2) letters to *The Times*, 13 February 1991, 7 January 1992, 14 July 1992.

London Business School (various years) *Economic Outlook*.

London Business School (various years) *Sunday Times*.

Manchester University (various years) *Manchester School*.

Matthews, K. (1995) 'Review of *Money, Credit and Asset Prices*', *Economic Affairs*, vol. 15, no. 3, Institute of Economic Affairs, London.

Mills, T. C. and Pepper, G. (1997) 'Assessing the Forecasters: An Analysis of the Forecasting Records of the Treasury, the LBS and the National Institute', *Economic Research Paper*, no. 97/9, Loughborough University.

Monetary Bulletin (various years) W. Greenwell & Co., London.

Monetary Control (1980) Cmnd. 7858, HMSO, London.

National Income Accounts (various years) Central Statistical Office, London.

National Institute Quarterly Review (various years) National Institute of Economic and Social Research, London.

Niehens, Jürg (1981) 'The Appreciation of Sterling – Causes, Effects and Policies', Money Study Group, SSRC, London.

North Holland (various years) *Economic Forecasts*, London.

Pepper, G. (1970) 'The Money Supply, Economic Management and the Gilt-edged market', *Journal of the Institute of Actuaries*, vol. 96, pp. 1–24.

Pepper, G. (1981) 'Behaviour of Financial Markets', *The Treasurer*, Association of Corporate Treasurers, London, February, pp. 9–14.

Pepper, G. (1990a) 'Monetary Policy, A Post-mortem and Proposal', Mais Lecture, City University Business School, London.

Pepper, G. (1990b) 'Money, Credit and Inflation', Institute of Economic Affairs, Research Monograph no. 44, London.

Pepper, G. (1992–4) 'Monitoring the Money Supply and Distortions to Monetary Data', Money, Macro and Finance Research Group, ESRC, 1992, and *National Westminster Bank Quarterly Review*, February 1993.

Pepper, G. (1994) *Money, Credit and Asset Prices*, Macmillan, London.

Pepper, G. (1993) 'Supply-Side Control of the Money Stock', Money, Macro and Finance Research Group, ESRC, 1993.

Pepper, G. and Wood, G. (1976) 'Too Much Money...?', Institute of Economic Affairs, Hobart Paper no. 68, London.

Radcliffe Report (1959) Committee on the Workings of the Monetary System, Cmnd. 827, HMSO, London.

Rose, H. (1960) *Economic Background to Investment,* Cambridge University Press, Cambridge.

Social Science Research Council (1981) Report by the Sub-Committee on Macro-Economic Research in the United Kingdom, London.

Thatcher, M. (1995) *Path to Power*, HarperCollins, London.

Treasury, HM (various years) *Autumn Statement.*

Treasury, HM (various years) *Economic Progress Report.*

Treasury, HM (varous years) *Financial Statement and Budget Report.*

Treasury, HM (1991) 'Memorandum on Official Economic Forecasting', Treasury & Civil Service Committee, Session 1990/1, *House of Commons Paper*, 532-(i), pp. 43–7.

Treasury, HM (various years) *Summer Economic Forecast.*

Walters, A. (various years in the 1970s) *Sebag Gilt Edged Review*, Joseph Sebag, London.

Walters, A. (1986) *Britain's Economic Renaissance: Margaret Thatcher's Reforms 1979–1984*, Oxford University Press, New York and Oxford.

Walters, A. (1990) *Sterling in Danger*, Fontana/Collins/Institute of Economic Affairs, London.

Wass, D. (1978) Johnian Society Lecture, *Economic Trends*, Central Statistical Office, London, no. 293, March.

Wilson, H. (1980) *Report of the Committee to Review the Functioning of Financial Institutions*, HMSO, London.

Glossary

The definitions of the monetary aggregates have changed from time to time. The ones given below were in force at the time the Monetary Bulletins were written. In the interest of simplicity some detail is omitted.

Sectors of the Economy

The sectors of economy are:
    public sector
    banking sector
    non-bank private sector
      personal sector
      corporate sector (including industrial and commercial companies)
    overseas sector

Flow of Funds

Each sector has a financial surplus or deficit *vis-à-vis* the rest of the economy. A sector reacts to its financial position, for example, it retrenches if there is an unusually large deficit.

Counterparts of Broad Money

The 'counterparts' of broad money are contained in the following identity (an identity is an equation that is correct by definition, as explained in Chapter 5, p. 47).

public sector borrowing requirement

plus

bank lending to the private sector

less

sales of gilt-edged stock and other public sector debt to the non-bank private sector

less

external financing of the public and banking sectors (including changes in the foreign exchange reserves)

less

growth of banks' non-deposit liabilities

equals
M3

Monetary Aggregates

The monetary aggregates are listed below in order of broadness:

M0
   banks' balances with the Bank of England plus their till money (vault cash) and notes and coin in circulation with the public

Retail M1 (Greenwell definition)
   M1 less wholesale overnight interest-bearing sight deposits

nibM1 (non-interest-bearing M1)
   M1 less accounts on which interest is payable

M1
   currency in circulation with the public plus current accounts (demand deposits) and sight deposits

M2
   sterling M3 less large wholesale deposits

Definitions before 1987:

sterling M3
   M1 plus deposit accounts (time deposits) but excluding deposits denominated in foreign currencies

M3
   sterling M3 plus foreign currency deposits

PSL1
   sterling M3 plus the non-bank private sector's holdings of bills (traded in the money market, for example commercial bills)

PSL2
   PSL1 plus building society deposits

Domestic credit expansion, DCE
   M3 without deduction for the external financing of the public and banking sectors. (A fall in the UK's foreign exchange reserves provides the public sector with finance – the government is in effect financing itself by selling foreign exchange – and this reduces the growth of M3. DCE corrects for such a reduction. It is the IMF's preferred measure for a country in balance of payments difficulties.)

Definitions after 1987:

M3
   M1 plus sterling deposit accounts (the old sterling M3)

M4
   M3 plus building society deposits

M5
   M4 plus bills (the old PSL2)

Monetary base control
   The Bank of England is banker to commercial banks. As such it is the ultimate supplier of liquidity upon which all banks have to rely and over which it has a monopoly. The Bank is in a position to ration supply. In more detail, the components of the monetary base (M0) are all liabilities of the Bank. Advocates of monetary base control argue that the Bank could control the monetary base if it controlled the size of its balance sheet and that it could do so by deciding on the amount of treasury and commercial bills that it purchased or sold each day on the money market. This is in contrast to the present system under which the Bank stands ready to deal in whatever quantity of bills banks want, determining the price (that is, the rate of interest at which it gives assistance) rather than the quantity of assistance.

Efficient-Market Hypothesis

The hypothesis states that markets are efficient in the sense that prices are such that profits cannot be made using existing available information. It follows that prices only alter when unexpected new information becomes available that alters investors' expectations of what the return on the share or shares is likely to be.

International Monetarism

This is explained in Section 2.11, p. 13 and in Section A. 9.1.4, pp. 14–15.

Exchange Rate Mechanism of the European Monetary System

This is the mechanism under which member countries agree to keep their currencies within bands.

Debt-deflation

After a financial bubble bursts and asset prices crash the value of collateral can easily fall below the amount of the loan it is securing (for example, negative equity on a house). People can then start to go bankrupt and retrenchment becomes enforced.

The extreme case of debt-deflation was illustrated in the US after the 1929 crash when banks had to call in loans because bad debts had wiped out their capital. The result was further sales of assets, the prices of which fell by even more, and another round of bankruptcies. The final stage was banks failing, depositors losing their money and the money supply collapsing. The outcome was a severe depression.

In the least worst case of debt-deflation, banks merely become wary about lending and borrowers become very cautious. Bank lending to the private sector then turns sluggish, as does monetary growth. The result is a prolonged recession.

Names Index

Subject Index